Protecting our Privacy

ISSUES

Volume 82

Editor

Craig Donnellan

WITHDRAWN

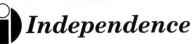

Independence

Educational Publishers
Cambridge

First published by Independence
PO Box 295
Cambridge CB1 3XP
England

British Library Cataloguing in Publication Data
Protecting our Privacy– (Issues Series)
I. Donnellan, Craig II. Series
323.4'48

ISBN 1 86168 277 8

Printed in Great Britain
MWL Print Group Ltd

Typeset by
Claire Boyd

Cover
The illustration on the front cover is by
Pumpkin House.

CONTENTS

Chapter One: The Privacy Debate

Chapter Two: Your Privacy Rights

Introduction

Protecting our Privacy is the eighty-second volume in the **Issues** series. The aim of this series is to offer up-to-date information about important issues in our world.

Protecting our Privacy looks at the privacy rights debate and our rights to privacy.

The information comes from a wide variety of sources and includes:
Government reports and statistics
Newspaper reports and features
Magazine articles and surveys
Web site material
Literature from lobby groups
and charitable organisations.

It is hoped that, as you read about the many aspects of the issues explored in this book, you will critically evaluate the information presented. It is important that you decide whether you are being presented with facts or opinions. Does the writer give a biased or an unbiased report? If an opinion is being expressed, do you agree with the writer?

Protecting our Privacy offers a useful starting-point for those who need convenient access to information about the many issues involved. However, it is only a starting-point. At the back of the book is a list of organisations which you may want to contact for further information.

*****

Nothing to hide, nothing to fear?

Dr Caoilfhionn Gallagher, Liberty's researcher on the Nuffield-funded privacy project, provides an overview of some recent Government measures which threaten our right to privacy.

When we hear the phrases 'right to privacy' or 'invasion of privacy', we usually think either of stories and photographs splashed across the front pages of the tabloid press – of a footballer visiting a brothel or having an affair, a supermodel attending a Narcotics Anonymous meeting, a celebrity cavorting naked on her honeymoon – or of oddball conspiracy theorists convinced that everyone is out to get them, determined to collect their post from PO boxes under assumed names, never use a computer and only eat food they have grown themselves. If you are not one of these people, or a terrorist or criminal, you may well ask, 'Why should I worry about my privacy? I have nothing to hide.'

This idea, that only the mad, bad or famous need worry about their privacy, is wrong-headed, but unfortunately it has taken root in Britain. When David Blunkett talks about ID cards, CCTV or mass surveillance of all citizens' e-mails and telephone calls, he talks about this idea of 'nothing to hide, nothing to fear'. When proposals to 'barcode babies', to create a permanent file with DNA and other information on every child in the country, are discussed, it is assumed that only child sex abusers will be affected, and not the ordinary, honest, law-abiding citizen.

> *If you are not one a terrorist or criminal, you may well ask, 'Why should I worry about my privacy? I have nothing to hide'*

Is this right? Do only the guilty have something to hide and something to fear from increased tracking, surveillance and monitoring by government? In fact, we all have something to hide – and not because we are doing anything wrong or breaking any laws, but because we are all entitled to private space, away from prying eyes and eavesdropping technologies. When someone reads a book over your shoulder on a bus, you will probably feel irritated, not because you are reading something smutty, but because your private space and choices are being intruded upon. When you go home at night and pull your curtains closed, you may not be doing anything wrong – the curtains may be concealing nothing more racy than dinner-eating and TV-watching – but it is your business and not that of the outside world.

Besides, the Government should surely assume that the average citizen has nothing to hide – and so shouldn't treat us all as if we are hiding something. Mass surveillance technologies do treat us all as suspects and not citizens. In 1932 an MP in the House of Commons spoke of 'the modern spirit of "nosey-parkerism" in legislation and administration'. Seventy years later this spirit of nosey-parkerism lives on.

In recent months there have been a number of developments which undermine the right to privacy, and reinforce the fact that the British public are the most spied-upon people in the Western world.

Communications data: a snoopers' charter?

'Communications data' or 'comms data' does not include the content of communications, but covers traffic data, location data and subject data – in other words, who you called, when you called, how long you talked for, and where you were when you called. It is possible to build up a detailed profile of a person from this type of information.

In June 2002 the Home Office was forced to retreat from its plans to greatly expand the public bodies entitled to monitor citizens' comms data. The plans were dubbed a 'snoopers' charter'. David Blunkett admitted he had 'got it wrong' and would need to 'think again and consult widely' before returning to Parliament with any new Orders.

After a year-long PR exercise by the Home Office, new Orders were put before Parliament in September 2003 – but they make the same mistakes as the old, disgraced Orders.

Two main Orders deal with comms data

The first is the Regulation of Investigatory Powers (Communications Data) Order 2003. It is designed to 'bring within the regulatory regime public authorities using communications data now without any regulation', according to the Home Office – but the Home Office should be asking whether it is right that they use these data, not simply legally rubber-stamping what they are doing already without legal cover.

The second Order is the Retention of Communications Data (Code of Practice) Order 2003. This introduces a 'voluntary' code of practice for internet and telephone service providers to retain details of their customers' data for Home Office purposes, but the Home Office has now decided to convert this 'voluntary' scheme to a mandatory one as soon as possible.

Directed surveillance and covert human intelligence sources

David Blunkett has also recently laid the Regulation of Investigatory Powers (Directed Surveillance and Covert Human Intelligence Sources) Order 2003 before Parliament. This remarkable Order allows new public bodies to use undercover agents and informants for investigations. The Charity Commission, the Gaming Board and the Postal Services Commission have all been granted these astounding powers. This is a particularly worrying development for organisations like Liberty (with a charitable sister) which work to promote human rights and campaign against certain Government policies. Ten years ago Liberty staff members Patricia Hewitt and Harriet Harman had to go to Strasbourg to prove that the British Government had no right to spy on them – and now the Home Secretary is allowing it to happen again. He says the Order is needed to regulate what public bodies are already doing – but he doesn't explain why it is just and proportionate for them to be doing so in the first place.

ID cards

Liberty members will know that David Blunkett's affection for national identity cards is long-standing. Since September 2001, in

the wake of the terrorist attacks in the US, the Home Secretary has presented them as the answer to a range of society's ills: terrorism, identity fraud, and now, finally, illegal immigration. His latest proposals at least admit that an ID card scheme would be compulsory, and not voluntary as suggested during the consultation process last year. The cost for his dream scheme is estimated at somewhere between £3 and £5 billion.

Of course, if the stated aim of the cards is to tackle illegal immigration, a racist impact is inevitable. If the police are to challenge people who look like illegal immigrants to produce their card to prove their entitlement to be in the country, who are they likely to stop? Middle-class white people? Or ethnic minorities? Evidence from France (where cards are not compulsory but over 90% of the population carries one) suggests that the North African community has been targeted disproportionately by the police. Our own experience of stop-and-search policing during the 1980s is hardly a good precedent, either.

The Home Secretary is hoping that ID cards will feature in the Queen's speech at the end of November. He will have been pleased by Tony Blair's suggestion in his Labour Party conference speech that the time may now be right to consider them. However, objections from leading members of the Cabinet may stymie his plans. Peter Hain, the leader of the Commons, Patricia Hewitt, the trade secretary, Charles Clarke, the education secretary, and Gordon Brown have all expressed concerns. Even Jack Straw, the foreign secretary, has written to cabinet colleagues warning of a 'large-scale debacle' and a huge public backlash if the plans are included in the Queen's speech. Straw himself proposed a national ID card scheme to the Cabinet in 1998 when he was Home Secretary, but eventually decided to drop the idea and use the money to recruit extra police officers instead.

National population computer database

The Cabinet's Public Expenditure

Committee, chaired by Gordon Brown, has recently endorsed preparatory work to go ahead on the creation of a national population computer database which could be used as the foundation stone for an ID card scheme.

Closed circuit television (CCTV)

The UK still has the highest density of CCTV cameras in the world. Since 1994 the Home Office has spent 78% of its crime prevention budget on CCTV, and there are now over 1.5 million cameras across the country.

CCTV has grown significantly from being used by companies to protect property and prevent shoplifting to becoming a tool used by law enforcement authorities for routine surveillance of public spaces. Video cameras are becoming smaller and more ubiquitous. CCTV technology has been described as 'the fifth utility' by some commentators who believe that it is being integrated into the urban environment in much the same way as the electricity supply and the telephone network were integrated in the first half of the twentieth century.

In most cases, cameras are hidden from view or disguised so as to be undetected by those passing by the camera's gaze; some cameras can swivel to locate someone and zoom in. Many Central Business Districts in Britain are now covered by surveillance systems involving a linked network of cameras with full pan, tilt, zoom and night vision or infrared capability.

Facial recognition technology

Facial recognition technology uses computerised matching technology to automatically identify people's faces.

Again, the UK is a world leader: the borough of Newham first deployed a facial recognition system to scan faces against a database to identify people 'of interest'. A form of this technology was famously used at the 2001 Super Bowl in Tampa, Florida, to compare the faces of those in the crowd to faces in a database of mug shots. There was widespread public outcry at this surveillance of

The UK still has the highest density of CCTV cameras in the world. Since 1994 the Home Office has spent 78% of its crime prevention budget on CCTV

unsuspecting attendees, prompting some to dub the event the 'Snooper Bowl'. This technology is becoming more popular in Britain and national trials are under way.

Air travel privacy

It is not only the British Government which threatens our privacy: since 9/11, the US Government is determined to do so too. Several measures have been introduced by the Bush administration to improve aviation security. Some of these proposals (improved training for airport screeners, strengthening cockpit doors) are sound security measures. The passenger data disclosure rules, however, present privacy and security risks.

The US has demanded that all international airlines provide the US Government with full electronic

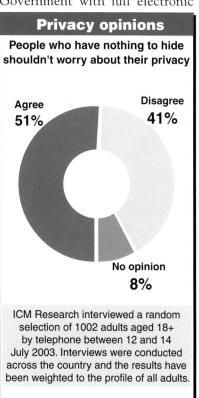

Privacy opinions

People who have nothing to hide shouldn't worry about their privacy

Agree **51%**

Disagree **41%**

No opinion **8%**

ICM Research interviewed a random selection of 1002 adults aged 18+ by telephone between 12 and 14 July 2003. Interviews were conducted across the country and the results have been weighted to the profile of all adults.

Source: Guardian Newspapers Limited 2003

access to detailed airline passenger data on all travellers. These data include name, address, flight number, credit card number, and choice of meal. The core idea is to use this information to focus security resources on suspicious travellers, while ensuring that most people are not inconvenienced by heightened security. In practice, this system targets particular ethnic groups and nationalities. Besides, there is no proof whatsoever that it is effective. Terrorists have, of course, been known to go to great lengths to look like most people. Former US Transportation Security Agency chief John Magaw refused to endorse a 'trusted traveller' card, fearing that it would be the first thing a terrorist would try to obtain.

The European Commission at first rejected US demands for this passenger information outright, saying these measures would breach EU data protection rules. While searching for a compromise, an interim arrangement has been reached – the EU has guaranteed not to enforce data protection laws until a new agreement is reached; in return, the US will give clarifications about how they will handle the data.

As the Home Secretary himself has put it, deciding the correct balance between respect for privacy and protecting the public 'is an issue for all of us, and it is important to get it right'. He must put this sentiment into practice.

Of course, it is not only governments that are interested in tracking and surveillance. Private sector companies, particularly supermarkets, and individuals also have an interest in knowing what we are up to. In the next issue of *Liberty* Caoilfhionn will review private sector technological developments. In the meantime, visit the privacy pages on our website www.liberty-human-rights.org.uk to keep up to date.

■ This article is the first of a two-parter from *Liberty*, the magazine by Liberty. Visit Liberty's web site at www.liberty-human-rights.org.uk Alternatively, see their address details on page 41.

© *Liberty*

Privacy and human rights

Information from Privacy International

Defining privacy

Privacy is a fundamental human right. It underpins human dignity and other values such as freedom of association and freedom of speech. It has become one of the most important human rights of the modern age.[1]

Privacy is recognised around the world in diverse regions and cultures. It is protected in the Universal Declaration of Human Rights, the International Covenant on Civil and Political Rights, and in many other international and regional human rights treaties. Nearly every country in the world includes a right of privacy in its constitution. At a minimum, these provisions include rights of inviolability of the home and secrecy of communications. Most recently written constitutions include specific rights to access and control one's personal information. In many of the countries where privacy is not explicitly recognised in the constitution, the courts have found that right in other provisions. In many countries, international agreements that recognise privacy rights such as the International Covenant on Civil and Political Rights or the European Convention on Human Rights have been adopted into law.

Of all the human rights in the international catalogue, privacy is perhaps the most difficult to define.[2] Definitions of privacy vary widely according to context and environment. In many countries, the concept has been fused with data protection, which interprets privacy in terms of management of personal information.

Outside this rather strict context, privacy protection is frequently seen as a way of drawing the line at how far society can intrude into a person's affairs.[3] The lack of a single definition should not imply that the issue lacks importance. As one writer observed, 'in one sense, all human rights are aspects of the right to privacy'.[4]

Some viewpoints on privacy

In the 1890s, future United States Supreme Court Justice Louis Brandeis articulated a concept of privacy that urged that it was the individual's 'right to be left alone'. Brandeis argued that privacy was the most cherished of freedoms in a democracy, and he was concerned that it should be reflected in the Constitution.[5]

Robert Ellis Smith, editor of the *Privacy Journal*, defined privacy as 'the desire by each of us for physical space where we can be free of interruption, intrusion, embarrassment, or accountability and the attempt to control the time and manner of disclosures of personal information about ourselves'.[6]

According to Edward Bloustein, privacy is an interest of the human personality. It protects the inviolate personality, the individual's independence, dignity and integrity.[7]

According to Ruth Gavison, there are three elements in privacy: secrecy, anonymity and solitude. It is a state which can be lost, whether through the choice of the person in that state or through the action of another person.[8]

The Calcutt Committee in the United Kingdom said that, 'nowhere have we found a wholly satisfactory statutory definition of privacy'. But the committee was satisfied that it would be possible to define it legally and adopted this definition in its first report on privacy:

'The right of the individual to be protected against intrusion into his personal life or affairs, or those of his family, by direct physical means or by publication of information.'[9]

The Preamble to the Australian Privacy Charter provides that, 'A free and democratic society requires respect for the autonomy of individuals, and limits on the power of both state and private organizations to intrude on that autonomy . . . Privacy is a key value which underpins human dignity and other key values such as freedom of association and freedom of speech . . . Privacy is a basic human right and the reasonable expectation of every person.'[10]

Aspects of privacy

Privacy can be divided into the following separate but related concepts:

Information privacy, which involves the establishment of rules governing the collection and handling of personal data such as credit information, and medical and government records. It is also known as 'data protection';

Bodily privacy, which concerns the protection of people's physical selves against invasive procedures such as genetic tests, drug testing and cavity searches;

Privacy of communications, which covers the security and privacy of mail, telephones, e-mail and other forms of communication; and

Territorial privacy, which concerns the setting of limits on intrusion into the domestic and other environments such as the workplace or public space. This includes searches, video surveillance and ID checks.

Models of privacy protection

There are four major models for privacy protection. Depending on their application, these models can be complementary or contradictory. In most countries reviewed in the survey, several are used simultaneously. In the countries that protect privacy most effectively, all of the models are used together to ensure privacy protection.

Comprehensive laws

In many countries around the world, there is a general law that governs the collection, use and dissemination of personal information by both the public and private sectors. An oversight body then ensures compliance. This is the preferred model for most countries adopting data protection laws and was adopted by the European Union to ensure compliance with its data protection regime. A variation of these laws, which is described as a 'co-regulatory model', was adopted in Canada and Australia. Under this approach, industry develops rules for the protection of privacy that are enforced by the industry and overseen by the privacy agency.

Sectoral laws

Some countries, such as the United States, have avoided enacting general data protection rules in favour of specific sectoral laws governing, for example, video rental records and financial privacy. In such cases, enforcement is achieved through a range of mechanisms. A major drawback with this approach is that it requires that new legislation be introduced with each new technology so protections frequently lag behind. The lack of legal protections for individuals' privacy on the Internet in the United States is a striking example of its limitations. There is also the problem of a lack of an oversight agency. In many countries, sectoral laws are used to complement comprehensive legislation by providing more detailed protections for certain categories of information, such as tele-communications, police files or consumer credit records.

Privacy is a fundamental human right. It underpins human dignity and other values such as freedom of association and freedom of speech

---

Self-regulation

Data protection can also be achieved, at least in theory, through various forms of self-regulation, in which companies and industry bodies establish codes of practice and engage in self-policing. However, in many countries, especially the United States, these efforts have been disappointing, with little evidence that the aims of the codes are regularly fulfilled. Adequacy and enforcement are the major problem with these approaches. Industry codes in many countries have tended to provide only weak protections and lack enforcement.

Technologies of privacy

With the recent development of commercially available technology-based systems, privacy protection has also moved into the hands of individual users. Users of the Internet and of some physical applications can employ a range of programs and systems that provide varying degrees of privacy and security of communications. These include encryption, anonymous remailers, proxy servers and digital cash.[11] Users should be aware that not all tools effectively protect privacy. Some are poorly designed while others may be designed to facilitate law enforcement access.

References:

1   Marc Rotenberg, *Protecting Human Dignity in the Digital Age* (UNESCO 2000).
2   James Michael, *Privacy and Human Rights* 1 (UNESCO 1994).
3   Simon Davies, *Big Brother: Britain's Web of Surveillance and the New Technological Order* 23 (Pan 1996).
4   Fernando, Volio, 'Legal personality, privacy and the family' in Henkin (ed), *The International Bill of Rights* (Columbia University Press 1981).
5   Samuel Warren and Louis Brandeis, The Right to Privacy, 4 *Harvard Law Review* 193-220 (1890).
6   Robert Ellis Smith, *Ben Franklin's Web Site* 6 (Sheridan Books 2000).
7   Privacy as an Aspect of Human Dignity, 39 *New York University Law Review* 971 (1964).
8   Privacy and the Limits of Law, 89 *Yale Law Journal* 421, 428 (1980).
9   Report of the Committee on Privacy and Related Matters, Chairman David Calcutt QC, 1990, Cmnd. 1102, London: HMSO, at 7.
10 *The Australian Privacy Charter*, published by the Australian Privacy Charter Group, Law School, University of New South Wales, Sydney (1994).
11 EPIC maintains a list of privacy tools at http://www.epic.org/privacy/tools.html

■ The above information is an extract from *Privacy and Human Rights 2003*, a report by Privacy International: www.privacyinternational.org Alternatively, see their address details on page 41.

© *Privacy International*

Watching them, watching us

UK public CCTV Surveillance regulation campaign

The United Kingdom leads the world in the deployment of closed circuit television camera technology. However, we seem to have no coherent, legally enforceable rules or regulations which ensure that public CCTV schemes are run properly.

This information aims to open up a debate about the extent to which powerful technologies such as linked CCTV camera systems, neural network facial recognition, car number plate recognition, multi-media image databases etc. are being applied in the UK.

Will David Blunkett and the new New Labour government be any more sensitive to civil liberties and privacy issues than Jack Straw and his Tory predecessors as Home Secretary were?

Why, in the UK, is television reception controlled by licences, backed up by criminal penalties, but no licensing is required to install linked CCTV camera systems?

Are CCTV surveillance systems vital to keep order on our streets, or are there substantial civil liberties problems to be addressed? Has the cost effectiveness of public CCTV surveillance systems been oversold? Is crime reduced or just displaced next door?

Are the existing schemes properly funded and coordinated with radio links to police or security patrols? Or is one operator meant to monitor over 50 cameras for a 12-hour shift on his own? Have the number of 'bobbies on the beat' been reduced as a result of the 'cost savings' of CCTV technology?

Do you want CCTV images of yourself sold to broadcast TV and video companies, without your permission, and without paying any royalties to you? Where CCTV images are used as evidence of crime,

are there proper procedures to prevent unauthorised editing or tampering with the evidence? Is it right that CCTV systems can automatically tag your behaviour in a public place as 'suspicious'?

What are the criteria for removal of suspects' images in facial recognition or video ID parade databases? Are they entered for the duration of an investigation, or are you branded as a suspect for life, in the same way as DNA databases seem to be abused?

Why, in the UK, is television reception controlled by licences, backed up by criminal penalties, but no licensing is required to install linked CCTV camera systems?

Will the results of facial recognition analysis e.g. number of women, numbers of whites, Asians or blacks walking down the street, be sold to marketing companies, or handed over to racists?

Should your car number plate be automatically read, recognised and logged? Will this lead to private 'burbclaves' or 'no-go areas'? Where are the safeguards to prevent foreign or UK intelligence agencies, terrorists, criminals or paparazzi journalists from gaining access to the individual vehicle traffic movement patterns of police cars, nuclear weapons or waste convoys, high value freight cargoes or VIPs?

Should 'in your face' policing be allowed to include video cameras aimed, especially at public

demonstrations, literally in people's faces, to intimidate people, when no actual offences have been committed?

Would you support criminal prosecution of those who abuse surveillance technologies, including those currently hiding behind Crown immunity?

Should CCTV surveillance regulation become the model for the control of other technologies, including millimetre wave radar, thermographic imaging and bio-sensors?

Does the judgement by the European Court of Human Rights show that all UK CCTV systems currently breach Article 8 of the European Declaration of Human Rights?

Why does the controversial Regulation of Investigatory Powers Act 2000 not attempt to regulate CCTV surveillance in any way?

When is a CCTV system a covert surveillance device which is covered by the RIP Act?

Does an overt CCTV system become a covert one if, like many systems, it is used to see beyond the range of normal human vision or in the dark?

Should CCTV images be published of people who are merely possible indirect witnesses (not the victims or the criminals), as they have been in recent murder investigations?

Should there be a minimum period for Data Retention of CCTV video and digital data? Is post-incident Data Preservation adequate? Should either of these be legally mandatory? Should the Government pay for the extra costs involved?

■ The above information is from the Watching Them, Watching Us web site: www.spy.org.uk

© *Watching Them, Watching Us*

ID cards may be Blair's 'plastic poll tax'

A large majority think they are a good idea, but a small group of passionate opponents could prove to be politically lethal, reports Anthony King

Any attempt to introduce a system of national identity cards could land the Government in deep trouble, according to YouGov's survey for the *Telegraph*.

The survey's headline figures showing a large majority in favour of such a system conceals depths of potentially lethal opposition. Identity cards have already been dubbed 'the Poll Tax in plastic'. They could turn out to be just that.

On the face of it, YouGov's findings appear paradoxical. Most Britons say they would welcome or at least not mind identity cards. In addition, most appear optimistic that they would reduce 'health tourism', benefit fraud and make it easier for police and other government agencies to apprehend criminals and identify bogus asylum seekers.

Yet at the same time large majorities believe that the system would be open to abuse and that personal details held on people's ID cards would probably be leaked to unauthorised people outside the Government.

Large majorities also believe that criminals would soon find ways of forging the cards and few voters reckon that the fee to be charged for acquiring a card, currently estimated to be about £40, is remotely reasonable. Most people think there should be no charge at all.

Perhaps most serious of all from the Government's point of view, seven per cent – equivalent to more than three million people – would object strongly to the introduction of cards and absolutely refuse to own one. Those opposed to ID cards feel far more passionately than those in favour. Opposition is widespread among the young.

The obvious conclusion to draw from the findings is probably also the correct one: that most Britons rather

By Anthony King

like the idea of identity cards in principle but that many would object to them in practice.

If the Government were already unpopular for other reasons, the political costs of anti-card protests and non-compliance, even if temporary, could be devastating.

The section of the chart headed 'Initial responses' sets out YouGov's headline findings. More than three-quarters favour a system of national identity cards, with the old more enthusiastic than the young.

Of those in favour, roughly half believe that people should not only be required to possess a card but should have to carry it with them at all times. The other half reckons that people should retain the option of leaving the card at home when they go out.

People's reasons for favouring cards emerge clearly from the section headed 'The card's objectives'. Large majorities believe that compulsory ID cards would deter foreigners from coming to Britain for free NHS treatment and would cut down on illegitimate claims for welfare benefits.

In the eyes of the majority, ID cards would also make it easier for the authorities to track down bogus asylum seekers and people trying to evade deportation. Cards might also prove useful in the war on crime.

However, doubts start to creep in when people begin to compare how they think the cards should be used with how they think they would actually be used. The contrasts between the 'should happen' and 'will happen' columns in that part of the chart could hardly be more striking.

Large majorities believe the data encoded on the cards should be limited in scope and kept strictly confidential. But large majorities also believe that the encoded data would not be 'only enough to establish a person's identity' and that the data would almost certainly find their way into the hands of other government departments and even people outside government.

Twice as many (60 per cent) believe that a national system of ID cards would be 'likely to be abused' as believe that it would be used 'strictly in accordance with its stated purposes' (28 per cent).

In other words, large numbers of people suspect that today's credit card fraud would be matched by a new wave of identity card fraud.

Considerable numbers also suspect that police and other authorities would use compulsory cards to target not only criminals, benefit fraudsters and bogus asylum seekers but also racial and other minority groups and young people.

'Foreign-looking people' might also find themselves subject to scrutiny.

Doubts about the cards' integrity are even more widespread. Only a quarter believes the cards could be 'made so sophisticated they would be virtually impossible to forge'. Fully two-thirds, 60 per cent, believe realistic forgeries would soon be in circulation.

However, the political crunch for the Home Secretary and the Cabinet seems likely to lie in the financing. The Treasury wants it to be self-financing and a fee of £40 per card is currently mooted. But almost no one accepts that a £40 charge would be reasonable and a massive 86 per cent reckon that ID cards – like the NHS – should be 'free at the point of delivery'.

In addition, most people appear to remember some of the recent computer-generated administrative fiascos, involving among others, the Passport Office, the Child Support Agency and the Inland Revenue. Three-quarters reckon the introduction of ID cards would be accompanied by 'a lot of disruption and inconvenience'. Only a fifth believes the process would proceed 'smoothly and efficiently'.

More abstract issues of personal freedom appear less bothersome to most people. A large majority, 82 per cent, believes ID cards would not reduce their personal freedom at all (58 per cent) or would reduce their freedom but only to an acceptable extent (24 per cent).

That said, roughly one person in seven, 14 per cent, says ID cards would indeed encroach on their personal freedom 'to an unacceptable degree' and roughly one in four, 26 per cent, appears worried that compulsory cards would bring closer a 'Big Brother' state.

More ominously, the seven per cent hard core of potential ID 'refuseniks' is more than equalled by the 11 per cent who say that, if anti-ID protests did develop, they would 'sympathise with the protesters' and even consider joining in. These numbers are small as proportions of the total adult population but in absolute numbers are substantial.

Depending on the specific question asked, they total between three and six million people, a disproportionate number of them middle-class.

Moreover 67 per cent of those opposed, compared with only 35 per cent in favour, said they 'care a lot' about the issue. A tepid majority thus confronts a more fervent minority.

The findings undoubtedly demonstrate that there is a large majority in Britain in favour of ID cards but they also suggest the hostile minority could turn out to be hard to handle. YouGov elicited the opinions of 2,330 adults on line between Sept 2 and 4 2003.

The data have been weighted to conform to the demographic profile of British adults as a whole.

■ Anthony King is professor of government at Essex University
© *Telegraph Group Limited, London 2004*

YouGov poll

Initial responses

Are you in favour of, or opposed to, the introduction of national identity cards?

	All	Aged 18-44	Aged 45+
In favour	78%	73%	83%
Opposed to	15%	17%	12%
Don't know	7%	10%	5%

Which option would you favour?

It should be compulsory to own one and for everyone to have their card with them at all times	39%
It should be compulsory to own one but people should be able to leave it at home when they go out	42%
People should have the right to decide whether to have an identity card or not	18%
Don't know	2%

The card's objectives

Would identity cards help, or not help, to achieve the following objectives?

	Yes, would	No, would not	Don't know
Cut down on 'health tourism'	78%	14%	9%
Cut down on benefit fraud	82%	13%	5%
Make it easier for police to catch criminals	60%	26%	14%
Make it easier for police, other officials to catch bogus asylum seekers, others attempting to avoid deportation	80%	14%	6%

Target groups

If there were identity cards, which of the following groups should/would the police and other public authorities target?

	Should target	Would target
Known, suspected criminals	82%	79%
People alleged to be falsely claiming state benefits	82%	64%
Asylum-seekers	75%	69%
Football hooligans	68%	73%
Racial, other minority groups	13%	48%
Young people	7%	46%
Foreign-looking people	6%	37%
None of these/Don't know	10%	11%

What should and will happen?

If the Government goes ahead with identity cards, do you think . . . ?

	Should	Will
The cards should/will contain only enough information to establish a person's identity	65%	37%
The cards should/will contain other personal details such as people's health record, social security details, DNA profile and home address	30%	44%
Personal details on the cards should /will remain confidential to the government department involved	72%	13%
Personal details should/will remain confidential to government and not be passed to unauthorised persons outside government	91%	28%

Forgery

% agreeing with each statement

Cards could be made so sophicated that they would be virtually impossible to forge	25%
Criminals would quickly find ways of forging them	66%
Don't know	9%

The costs %

There is a suggestion that everyone will have to pay around £40 for their card. Do you think that . . . ?

Roughly £40 is a reasonable charge	1%
There should be a charge but £40 is too high	13%
There should not be any charge	86%
Don't know	1%

Freedom and protest

Which statement comes closest to your own view?

Identity cards would reduce my personal freedom to an unacceptable degree	14%
Identity cards would reduce my personal freedom but the benefits would outweigh the disadvantages	24%
Identity cards would not reduce my personal freedom at all	58%
Don't know	5%

Source: Telegraph YouGov poll, September 2003

The hi-tech ID card built into a passport

Blunkett beats off civil liberties opponents in his war on immigration

David Blunkett ushered in identity cards 'by the back door' yesterday with a scheme for expensive hi-tech passports and driving licences.

The documents required by every traveller and driver will double in price and store computerised images of the holder's face, fingerprints or eye, the Home Secretary announced.

Critics said the proposals – which will increase the cost of a passport from £42 to £77 and a driving licence from £31 to £73 – were noting more than an 'identity tax' and expressed concern over how the information on the cards would be used.

But Mr Blunkett said he had 'no sympathy at all' with the civil liberties argument. Unveiling his plans in the Commons he said ID cards were vital to tackle benefit abuse, illegal immigration and terrorism.

'Whether you choose to drive or whether you choose to have a passport is of course your decision,' he said.

'But whether you choose to fiddle public services, or to be here illegally and work illegally is not a choice that should be available.'

By James Chapman, Political Correspondent

The announcement represented apparent victory for Mr Blunkett in the fierce battle to push through his plan for ID cards. He was backed by the Prime Minister but opposed by Cabinet colleagues including Gordon Brown and Jack Straw, who predicted they would turn into an expensive and ultimately pointless assault on liberty.

> *The documents required by every traveller and driver will double in price and store computerised images of the holder's face, fingerprints or eye*

To mollify them, the crucial decision on whether to introduce compulsion has been postponed.

Under the Blunkett blueprint, everyone renewing their passport or driving licence will also get a built-in card carrying unique personal information.

A computer chip inside the card will store 'biometric' data, which could be face recognition, fingerprints or an iris scan. The Government plans eventually to set up a National Identity Register to hold details of all 60 million people in the UK. Information stored on ID cards could then be checked against the register to authenticate the holder's identity.

Because computer chips decay, it is expected they will have to be replaced every five years, though fees will be scaled down if this is the case.

A plain ID card, for those who do not have and do not want a driving licence or passport, will be available for around £35.

Under-16s will qualify for a free card, while retired people and those on low incomes will pay just £10.

The Home Office predicts that within ten years, eight out of every ten adults will be carrying ID cards.

The momentum to make them compulsory will then be unstoppable, Mr Blunkett believes.

Eventually, they would have to be produced to see a doctor, get a job or claim benefits.

Draft legislation to kickstart the process will be placed before Parliament next year.

The cost of the scheme is forecast at £180 million over the next three years, through the total is expected to reach £3billion after a decade.

It is hard to see how replacement driving licences every five years would not add significantly to the cost.

Traditionally, a licence is valid till the age of 70, after which it has to be renewed every three years. The Home Secretary insisted that ID cards were not a luxury or a whim but a 'necessity'.

'The implementation of this scheme will begin as soon as the legislative framework and technology have been put in place for the renewal of first passports, and then driving licences,' he said.

'I know some people believe there is a sinister motive behind the cards – that they will be a part of a Big Brother state.

'This is wrong. Only basic information will be held on the ID card database, such as your name, address, birthday and sex.

'It will not have details of religion, political beliefs, marital status or your health records.'

The final decision on which method of identity is used will depend in part on the choices made by other countries planning similar schemes.

Scientists say using the iris, the coloured part of the eye, is the most secure option.

The eye would be scanned when a card is issued, and then easily matched against computer records because the iris is totally unique.

David Davis, in his first outing as shadow home secretary, condemned Mr Blunkett's announcement as a feeble attempt to hide the fact that the Government is 'divided from top to bottom' on the issue.

'This is a compromise, a fudge and a massive deferral that does not address the huge problems of illegal immigration, fraud, organised crime and terrorism,' he said.

How it would work

Within four years all passport applicants will undergo face, fingerprint or iris scans and receive a hi-tech identity card built into their new document. A National Identity Register will be compiled containing details of all 60 million UK residents, which the cards can then be checked against.

The timescale

Set-up phase of three years before people start to get new hi-tech driving licences and passports. ID cards, for those who do not have or do not want a passport or a driving licence, would be introduced in 2007.

The technology

Cards will carry a photograph of the holder, plus a computer chip storing 'biometric' security features. The three options are fingerprints, iris scans or facial recognition technology. Face scans measure facial features that do not alter – such as distance between eyes. The 266 elements in each iris, can be quickly and easily scanned. No two irises are the same, even those of identical twins.

The cost

A combined passport and ID card will cost £77, a combined driving licence and ID card £73. A plain ID card will cost around £35. Foreign nationals will be charged the same amount for a card in the form of a resident's permit. Plain ID cards will be free for 16-year-olds, will cost around £10 over ten years for those on low incomes, and over-75s. The cost to the taxpayer will be £180 million over the first three years, rising to a forecast £3bn over the next decade.

Who gets it

Compulsory for everyone applying for or renewing a driving licence or passport. By 2013, this means 80 per cent of people will carry an ID card. The decision to make it compulsory for every citizen will be taken later this decade, and would have to be approved by Parliament. Under current plans, it will never be compulsory to carry a card at all times.

He asked what would happen if an illegal immigrant was asked to produce their card, given there are no plans to make it compulsory to carry one at all times.

The final decision on which method of identity is used will depend in part on the choices made by other countries planning similar schemes

---

The honest citizen, he said, would go to their local police station at a later date as requested.

'But the illegal immigrant will simply disappear,' he added.

Mr Blunkett's former Home Office ministerial colleague Barbara Roche joined in the criticism, warning that introduction of an ID card scheme would be chaotic.

'I think that there is a real issue of civil liberties and I am really not convinced that the cost implications of an exercise on this scale would really lead down the line to a really valuable weapon in the fight against crime and terrorism,' she said. 'All the evidence suggests that governments simply aren't very good at very big high-tech endeavours of this kind.'

Mark Oaten, Liberal Democrat home affairs spokesman, said: 'The scheme is unworkable and will cost millions, which would be better spent on reducing crime and making our streets safer.'

© *The Daily Mail*
November, 2003

Playing the ID card

Information from www.spiked-online.com

By Josie Appleton

The Home Secretary David Blunkett has unveiled plans to start issuing identity cards to millions of British citizens within three years, and to make the card compulsory within 10 years.[1]

As a practical policy to combat crime, illegal immigration or terrorism, these identity card proposals make very little sense. The plans only make sense as the product of a paranoid government that wants to get a handle on its population. The government wants to know for sure who people are. It doesn't seem to want to know for any particular reason or to achieve any particular end; it just wants to know.

Blunkett's White Paper, *Identity Cards: The Next Steps*, talks about the cards providing a 'secure form of personal identification'.[2] He worries that greater global mobility and advancing technology are making it 'increasingly difficult to protect and authenticate people's identity'. The information on the card – your name, address, photograph, iris pattern, and fingerprints – would be held on a National Identity Register, which would provide a 'single highly reliable record of a person's identity'.

Of course, every modern state wants to know who its citizens are, but these proposals border on the obsessive. The government's desire to know for certain who somebody is means that Britain may become the first country to use iris recognition as a way of identifying its citizens.

Running throughout the document is a preoccupation with anybody who might be trying to evade or deceive the state. The bogeymen that Blunkett conjures up to justify this policy are symbols as much as anything else.

Take the concern with 'identity theft', for example. Of course, some people steal credit card details to buy goods, or send spam email from false addresses – but identity cards are hardly a solution to this widespread electronic fraud, since you can't currently show your card (or your face) online. There are also those shady types who live, travel or launder money under aliases – but this is neither a new nor a common occurrence. The government seems to be concerned about identity theft, not because of the scale of the problem, but because of what it symbolises: someone trying to conceal their 'real' identity from the state.

More bizarrely, *Identity Cards: The Next Steps* suggests that identity cards will help forge individual and collective identities. A bit of plastic bearing vital statistics is here being attributed with a huge metaphysical power – to give individuals a secure sense of themselves and their place in the community. So the report says that cards will 'enable [individuals] to assert their identity and that they belong here'. The card will help to forge a more cohesive society, the report argues: 'It will show that everyone belongs to our society whether they were born here, have chosen to make their home here or are just staying for a while to study and work.'

What all this reflects is the government's sense of distance from the public. At a time when voting is at an all-time low, and public suspicion of politicians is at an all-time high, it is no surprise that the government feels that its citizens are, in effect, strangers. Hence the desire to establish with absolute certainty who people are – and the paranoid concern with those who are perceived as evading the clutches of the state.

ID cards represent a society where we are constantly having to answer for ourselves. The notion that people will band together around their ID cards is, however, fanciful. Civic pride and cohesion can't be issued by bureaucrats – such things come out of people's lives in their communities, and they involve issues more substantial than their iris patterns. And anybody who genuinely feels that their card allows them to 'assert their identity' is less a model citizen than a model patient for the men in white coats.

As Dolan Cummings has argued on *spiked*, Blunkett's proposals for ID cards are in effect trying to 'reconstitute the public as a membership organisation'. The government is trying to build a new civil society – a new kind of community that is tied directly to the state, rather than going about its unknown business. By issuing ID cards, the state gets to say who does and does not belong to the public. In return, the public is expected to show its commitment as a member of this ID-card community – forking out up to £77 a shot.

Blunkett has claimed that the cards will help to tackle illegal immigration and terrorism – but it is hard to see how. Knowing the names and fingerprints of everybody in the country won't stop terrorists – after all, the 9/11 hijackers lived openly under their own names in America and Germany. Identifying terrorists requires specific intelligence rather than general knowledge. Similarly, once they have entered the country, illegal immigrants would be able to evade ID card controls just as they do at present with existing checks on identity.

What does all this mean for our civil liberties? In immediate practical terms, not very much. ID cards will only contain very basic information – rather than data such as health, bank and tax records, as was previously suggested. Government agencies and the police will be restricted from accessing information from the National Identity Register – they will be able to verify someone's identity, but not much more. In addition, the police won't be able to stop an individual and demand to see his or her card.

What's more, the government has chosen such a timid way to phase in the cards that we probably won't notice much difference. In the first stage, ID cards will be issued in the place of people's passports and driving licences when they run out – and for everybody else, the cards will be optional. In 10 years, the government estimates that around 80 per cent of the population will be covered by this method – and so when the cards are eventually made compulsory, there won't be much of a fuss.

But the cards do represent an attack upon the culture of liberty – upon our sense that we can do as we please within the law, and mix freely with others. What ID cards represent is a society where we are constantly having to answer for ourselves – constantly having to say who we are, to prove our identity to officialdom. They also symbolise a society where we are mistrustful of our fellow citizens. In Blunkett-world, we should only trust those who have become a member of the ID-card community, and are allowing the powers that be to keep tabs on them.

When it comes down to it, the cost of ID cards will be far more than £77.

References
1 'Millions to get ID cards within 3 years', *The Times*, 12 November 2003
2 *Identity Cards: The Next Steps*, Home Office, November 2003

What is *spiked*?

spiked is an online publication with the modest ambition of making history as well as reporting it. *spiked* stands for liberty, enlightenment, experimentation and excellence: www.spiked-online.com

Biometric cards will not stop identity fraud

By Duncan Graham-Rowe

A plan to introduce biometric ID cards in the UK will fail to achieve one of its main aims, *New Scientist* has learned. The proposed system will do nothing to prevent fraudsters acquiring multiple identity cards.

Unveiling the proposals last week, the home secretary, David Blunkett, said they are necessary to prevent identity fraud. Every resident would have to carry an ID card containing biometric information, such as an iris scan. Cards could then be checked against a central database to confirm the holder's identity.

But Simon Davies, an expert in information systems at the London School of Economics and director of Privacy International, says the system would not stop people getting extra cards under different names. If he is correct, it could have far-reaching implications.

Other countries and organisations, including the International Civil Aviation Organisation, are planning to introduce similar ID schemes, and from October 2004 travellers to the US will require a biometric visa.

Limited accuracy

The problem, says Davies, is the limited accuracy of biometric systems combined with the sheer number of people to be identified. The most optimistic claims for iris recognition systems are around 99 per cent accuracy – so for every 100 scans, there will be at least one false match.

This is acceptable for relatively small databases, but the one being proposed will have some 60 million records. This will mean that each person's scan will match 600,000 records in the database, making it impossible to stop someone claiming multiple identities.

Even if they already had one or more records in the database, these would be swamped by the hundreds of thousands of false matches.

Lighting conditions

Davies sees no prospect of improvements to the technology solving the problem. Bill Perry, of the UK's Association for Biometrics, agrees that there is an upper limit to the reliability of iris scans. There are too many environmental variables: scans can be affected by lighting conditions and body temperature, so much so that a system can fail to match two scans of the same iris taken under different conditions.

'It's not an exact science,' says Perry. 'People look at biometrics as being a total solution to all their problems, but it's only part of the solution.'

A spokesman for the UK Home Office said: 'The UK Passport Service will be carrying out a trial very soon on enrolment procedures, and all these things will be looked at and measures taken to ensure that this will be a secure system.'

He added that using more than one biometric identifier – for example, iris scans and fingerprints together – will also be considered. This would solve the accuracy problem, but vastly increase the cost.

■ The above article is from a Special Report from the *New Scientist* Print Edition, 21 November 2003.

RFID

Frequently asked questions

Q. What is RFID?
A. Radio Frequency IDentification is an automatic data capture technology that uses tiny tracking chips affixed to products. These tiny chips can be used to track items at a distance – right through someone's purse, backpack, or wallet. Many of the world's largest manufacturing companies would like to replace the bar code with these 'spy chips', meaning that virtually every item on the planet – and the people wearing and carrying those items – could be remotely tracked. There is currently no regulation protecting consumers from abuse of this technology.

Q. What do RFID chips and tags look like?
A. RFID chips are usually attached to antennas. The chip and antenna combination is called a 'tag'. RFID tags vary widely in size, shape and colour.

Q. What companies make or use RFID devices?
A. We have a list of 103 companies that were sponsors of the MIT Auto-ID Center as of 25 June 2003. The MIT Auto-ID Center is the organisation developing the infrastructure for RFID with the help of global businesses like Gillette, Unilever and Procter & Gamble. We expect that these companies will be among the first to adopt the technology.

Q. How can I tell if there's an RFID chip in my . . . ?
A. Since no law requires manufacturers to tell you when they've put an RFID chip into a product or its packaging, the only way for an average consumer to know if a product contains a chip is to see it with his or her own eyes. (Or you can invest in an electronics lab and costly RFID readers.) The good news is that most RFID devices in commercial use today have a fairly conspicuous antenna, ranging from the size of a fingernail to the size of a full-sized sheet of paper.

RFID is an automatic data capture technology that uses tiny tracking chips affixed to products. These tiny chips can be used to track items at a distance

---

If you suspect that an item contains a hidden RFID chip, here are a few search tips:

- Look closely at any paper labels or stickers on the object. Peel them off and hold them up to the light. Do you see flat, dark or metallic lines converging on a central point? If so, you may be looking at the antenna of an RFID chip.

- The least invasive way to check for RFID chips in shoes is to pull back the inner pads and look around or have the shoes X-rayed. The problem with RFID chips is that they can be embedded in plastic, foam, rubber or other materials at the manufacturing plant. Short of destroying the shoes or having them X-rayed, it would be hard to find deeply embedded chips. We are still researching the use of RFID chips in shoes to determine the extent of any chipping. (See the Q & A on shoes below for more information.)

- If the item is made of cardboard, first scan its surface. Do you see a small, clear, flat plastic housing the size of a match head stuck anywhere onto the cardboard? If so, is it hooked up to a flat, metallic antenna or to matte grey spray-on ink? If so, you are most likely looking at an RFID tag. Pull the cardboard layers apart and look for a tell-tale antenna

embedded inside. It is rumoured that International Paper, an Auto-ID Center sponsor that makes packages for consumer goods, among other things, may be devising ways to embed RFID tags directly into paper and cardboard packaging.

- If you have access to an X-ray machine (say, if you're a veterinarian or a chiropractor) you can X-ray the item to see if it contains an RFID tag. Since most antennas are metal-based, you should be able to spot an RFID tag in this way.* Again, you are looking for an antenna converging on a central dot-sized chip. If you find something unusual and would like us to take a look, drop us an e-mail.

*Note that some highly advanced defence department and academic research chips do not have a 'tell-tale antenna' since they combine the antenna within the chip itself. These devices can be so small they would be nearly impossible to find.

Q. What do I do if I find an RFID chip? Can I kill or disable it?
A. You can disable a chip for all practical purposes by disconnecting it from its antenna. It is usually pretty obvious where the chip is located in an RFID tag (all the antennas will run to it). Once you find the tiny black square you can use a pair of scissors or a knife to cut it off.

To ensure that the tiny chip cannot later be read (assuming anyone could even find a device so small), you can puncture it with a straight pin, crush it, or pulverise it. (Note: While burning or micro-waving can destroy a chip, we do not recommend these methods because of fire risk. See the Q & A below.) Do not try to 'drown' it, since water does not generally destroy RFID chips. Running a magnet over the chip will not work, either.

Q. Can I microwave products to kill any hidden RFID tags they might contain?
A. While microwaving an RFID tag will destroy it (a microwave emits high frequency electromagnetic energy that overloads the antenna, eventually blowing out the chip), there is a good chance the tag will

burst into flames first. The difficulty of destroying a hidden RFID chip is one reason we need legislation making it illegal to hide a chip in an item in the first place.

Q. Are there some products that can't be RFID chipped?
A. Items containing LIQUID or METAL are especially hard to chip. Liquids tend to absorb the electromagnetic energy needed to power the chip, while metal tends to reflect it and bounce it around in unpredictable ways. Both problems can cause interference in the RFID signal sent by a chip to the reader. These bugs are still being worked on.

You can use this information about metal to your advantage. Has your store recently remodelled, replacing traditional metal shelving with new-fangled plastic shelves, to prevent interference with RFID transmission?

Q. Will a magnet erase an RFID chip?
A. No, the chips are not magnetically encoded. Running a magnet over

---

RFID chips are usually attached to antennas. The chip and antenna combination is called a 'tag'. RFID tags vary widely in size, shape and colour

---

the chip or using a tape eraser will not affect the chip.

Q. Can chips in clothing survive the washer and dryer?
A. Yes. They are designed to withstand years of normal wear and tear, including washing and drying. In fact, we know of at least one uniform rental company that uses RFID chips to keep track of its inventory. The chips hold up under the rough handling and commercial washings.

Q. Is it true they want to put RFID chips in Euro banknotes?
A. Hitachi has been working with the European Central Bank on the idea of putting RFID chips into Euro banknotes. This would eliminate the anonymity of cash by making it trackable. In essence, it would 'register' your cash to you when you get it from the teller or take it out of the ATM. Euro banknotes could be RFID tagged as early as 2005.

Q. Does US currency contain RFID chips?
A. To the best of our knowledge, US currency does NOT currently contain RFID chips.

Q. What's the read range of these chips? Can they be tracked by satellite?
A. There are two types of tags: 'passive' (no independent power source) and 'active' (containing a battery or attached to one). Depending on a number of factors (antenna size, RF frequency, environmental

conditions etc.) a passive tag can have a range of anywhere from 1 inch to 40 feet. Active tags can have a read range of miles or more. Most tags being considered for use in consumer products are passive.

Q. Is CASPIAN *aware of any RFID tags in shoes?*
A. We are aware of at least one company that uses embedded RFID technology in shoes for security purposes. According to the shoe company, the RFID labels they use do not contain unique product information. Rather, the RFID labels reportedly serve only to trigger an alarm if a consumer leaves the store without paying for the shoes. (Note that at a June 2003 RFID conference in Chicago, Alien Technology displayed a Wal-Mart Athletic Works® running shoe with an Alien RFID tag inserted under the insole. Alien said that the shoe was for display purposes only and that there were no planned/current trials or applications in those shoes. However, there was much excitement at the conference over the possibilities for RFID chips in shoes. Their stated reason for wanting to chip shoes was to keep shoe sizes together and match pairs. In our opinion, pervasive RFID chipping of shoes will become a frightening reality unless we tell companies that we will not buy products with chips!)

■ The above information is from Stop RFID's web site: www.spychips.com The Stop RFID website is a project of CASPIAN, Consumers Against Supermarket Privacy Invasion and Numbering.
© CASPIAN 2003-2004

Spy chips

An article on radio frequency identification (RFID) tags (aka spy chips). By Dr Susanne Lace, National Consumer Council

Introduction
This article explains what RFID tags are and provides some background to the debate about their use in the media.

What are RFID tags?
Tags are microchips with antennae that use wireless technology. They are embedded in goods or built into packaging and send signals in response to 'requests' from hand-held or door-mounted scanners (that may be located up to 17ft [5m] away). The scanner sends radio signals that wake up the tag, triggering it to respond by transmitting a unique code. Passive RFID tags can be as small as a grain of sand – at this size, they have no batteries and are powered by a scanner's signal. Larger tags have their own power and a greater transmission range.

Apparently, these tags were developed to track batches of products through the supply chain. However, the cost of tags has been falling. Currently, they cost around 20 to 50p but prices could fall to as little as 6p or less within three or four years. (NB Others think this would take over a decade to achieve.) Now the move is to tag individual products.

When individual products are tagged, the scanner links each product code to its own database entry which reveals what and where the product is. Other items of information could be added to this database entry, such as what the product cost and who bought it. This could be linked to other database information (such as store, loyalty or credit card data).

NCC National Consumer Council
Making all consumers matter

When individual products are tagged, the scanner links each product code to its own database entry which reveals what and where the product is

The Auto-ID Center (part of Massachusetts Institute of Technology in Boston) is developing a common standard that would allow tags to gain widespread adoption. It is supported by over 100 global companies and the US defence department. They are particularly bullish, stating that they are 'designing, building, testing and deploying a global infrastructure – a layer on top of the internet – that will make it possible for computers to identify any object anywhere in the world instantly'.

Why are tags gaining media coverage?
The UK is now at the forefront of trials of this technology.

Katherine Albrecht, director of the US organisation Consumers Against Supermarket Privacy Invasion and Numbering (CASPIAN), is also very active in gaining media coverage of the issue. She launched a boycott of Benetton and Gillette products after they trialled tags and is currently trying to set up a UK branch of CASPIAN.

Who is interested in tags and why?
Many organisations are using or thinking of using this technology, although reports do not always explain why:

Microsoft has announced that it will build RFID support into its software.

Transport for London is using RFID tags in its new Oyster travel cards – one aim is to improve passenger flow.

Timex is already selling an RFID-tagged watch that can automatically charge credit cards.

Michelin is planning to tag its tyres with chips that store a unique tyre number and associate the tyre with a Vehicle Registration Number.

Tesco has piloted use of tags, primarily for stock-control purposes but apparently also to prevent shoplifting. Tags were attached to Gillette razor-blade packaging and linked to cameras. Tags triggered a CCTV camera when the package was removed from the shelf and a second camera took a picture of the customer at the checkout. Security staff then compared the two images.

Marks and Spencer piloted the use of tags, attached to product labels, in their High Wycombe store in October 2003.

The European Central Bank is thinking about putting tags into bank notes, to combat forgery and to allow banks to count large amounts of cash in seconds.

John Radcliffe Hospital, Oxford, is considering using tags in its blood transfusion service.

The Home Office has ploughed £5.5 million into its 'Chipping of Goods' initiative and funded at least one of the Tesco trials. They believe that tagging will assist the police in identifying and recovering stolen property and will deter thieves. (Their arguments appear to work on the assumption that thieves will not get hold of tag disabling devices.)

Is the use of tags legal?

A unique product code could constitute 'personal data' under the Data Protection Act (DPA) if it is linked to personally identifiable customer information such as a store or credit card number. In this case, the usual rules of data protection would apply. Customers would have to consent to the use of the tag (so they would have to be told about the use of the tag and be given a clear opportunity in store to disable the tag). In relation to the photographs in the Tesco trial, to comply with the DPA there would have to be proper notification of data use to the Commissioner and rules about retention of the photographs etc.

Where RFID tags don't transmit personal data, the common law of confidence and the Human Rights Act might be used to protect privacy, but protection here is uncertain.

What are/might be the policy issues?

At present, there is a lot of confusion about how tags work and how they might be used and developed. Policy issues will also vary according to how tags are used. The following discussion is therefore necessarily tentative:

1. Privacy enhancing technology (PET)

It is currently unclear how far tags can be protected by PET – such as through encryption and by 'blocker tags' that consumers could use to stop scanners from working. One report, for example, has suggested that tags can be shielded from scanners 'with nothing more high tech than aluminium foil'! This needs to be explored.

2. In-store and out-of-store surveillance

Tags could be used as a covert (or overt) surveillance device. This may be to track possible shoplifters and/or to provide real-time research on customer behaviour.

If tags are not deactivated before a consumer leaves a store, it may be possible to monitor individuals

---

Tesco has piloted use of tags, primarily for stock-control purposes but apparently also to prevent shoplifting

---

through the radio signals their clothes or personal items continue to emit. The tagging of Michelin tyres raises the question of whether they now plan to track vehicle journeys? Chips could be also used at toll booths, to track vehicle journeys. One of the Oyster card's advertised aims is to 'provide better information about customers' travel patterns'. Through my own research, I've found out that the cards contain details of the last 8 journeys the holder made (accessible by London Transport staff with a reader – so they could find out [when cards are renewed] when people's homes are unoccupied). A central computer also contains details of journeys made in the last 2 months – I've not yet been able to find out whether those data are anonymised. If they are not, then agencies such as law enforcement and the Inland Revenue may be able to access details of the precise journeys people made.

The question also remains of whether tag deactivation might be possible when goods are delivered direct to a consumer's home.

CASPIAN are also concerned that tags will be linked to CCTV street cameras, but it is unclear whether this will be possible.

3. Possible consumer benefits

Some of the examples of how tags might be used suggest tangible consumer benefits. For example, many NHS hospital appointments are blighted by lost medical records; if tags were attached to patient records, these problems might be substantially reduced. Many other medical applications could also be developed (for example, to prevent medical accidents by linking patient information in tagged plastic bracelets to hospital prescribing systems).

Similarly, significant improvements could be made to postal services (on-line and mail order business might benefit, for instance, and the problem of credit card, cheque book and passport theft might be reduced). Consumer safety might also be improved, if tags help consumers and service providers spot unsafe counterfeit products. Another big potential advantage is the use of tags to improve consumer information – for example, if readers were widely available, consumers could read tags which could contain useful product information. Tags are also being developed to assist people with sight impairments to navigate their way around buildings and areas.

In relation to retail consumer goods, industry will argue that consumers will benefit from lower prices and permanently full shelves as stock will be managed more efficiently. Ultimately, the technology may replace check-out staff, as scanners could work out the price of goods and automatically debit credit cards – but would consumers want this and might this impact on credit card fraud?

Another questionable benefit is the use of tags to personalise marketing further. According to *Marketing Week* '[A] retailer could read details of the clothes worn and accessories carried by every customer as they enter a store. Linking information about a product to when and where it was bought would enable the retailer to discover the name, address and details of the person wearing it. The retailer could then use this information to make personalised offers to customers, for instance via a screen on their shopping trolley.'

(NB This is one step up from a central London department store which already uses facial recognition technology to alert staff to the entry of high-spending customers!)

The flip-side of this could be the exclusion of those who do not fit a desirable consumer profile, with possible discrimination on the price of goods (some stores in the US apparently already have two pricing systems – for those who do and don't own loyalty cards).

4. Function creep – information recorded for one purpose being used for another

If companies/organisations record the information captured by tags, it may be of interest to others, such as government departments and law enforcers. This again raises civil liberty issues. There is also the issue of inter and intra-company data-sharing, which can have exclusionary consequences. To quote the Auto-ID Center again, with this technology in place, 'you can get detailed profiles of customers for a certain geographical area or even as finely defined as a single store. If the same tag is used at other retail outlets, you can collect data of the same customer's buying patterns of other products.'

5. Crime

Will it be possible to read tags at a greater distance in future, with implications, for example, for potential burglars and unofficial police searches? If tags are not disabled (and scanners are stolen), the potential for theft may increase as wallets broadcast the amount of money they contain and homes broadcast their contents.

Retailers' databases would also be subject to the usual threats from hackers.

However, technological solutions to these problems might be developed. For example, researchers at Salford University are developing chips that trigger an alarm when high value items that are usually placed together in homes (such as TVs and DVD players) are separated.

6. Safety

Promoters of the technology appear convinced that it is safe. We need to find out more about this.

■ The above information is from the National Consumer Council. Visit their web site: www.ncc.org.uk Alternatively, see their address details on page 41.

Privacy and surveillance

Information from GreenNet Educational Trust (GET)

What is surveillance?

Surveillance is the monitoring of activities of an individual, group or groups of people. New opportunities for mass surveillance are opening up daily with high-speed, networked computers facilitating many of our everyday activities. Surveillance today may be carried out via the Internet, via telephone networks or via the data profiling of individuals. It is carried out for a variety of reasons – by the private sector for commercial ones (such as the protection of intellectual property rights), or by states for security reasons. Surveillance may be:

■ Passive – this analyses the trails of information generated by people's everyday activities. It usually focuses on patterns of activity and includes techniques such as:
– data profiling and dataveillance (often used for market research,

direct marketing or political lobbying)
– online monitoring of internet activity (for example, through data communications, information or cookies to track information on which websites are visited by an individual)
– enforcing intellectual property rights (through embedded information which tracks an individual's use of a particular software or online service)
■ Directed – this can usually only be used in certain circumstances relating to serious crime. It directly targets and monitors

specific individuals. It includes techniques such as:
– tapping communications (including internet data);
– bugging places of work;
– monitoring or infiltrating activities and networks through human agents.

How is surveillance covered by law?

Directed surveillance is covered by the Regulation of Investigatory Powers Act 2000,[1] and the Terrorism Act 2000.[2] They update the powers of the state to tap communications and to infiltrate networks or organisations. These laws require that:

■ any directed surveillance must be properly authorised by a person empowered to do so;

■ this authorisation must be subjected to scrutiny to ensure that it was justified under the relevant law, and that it was correctly applied.

Some kinds of directed surveillance controls are enabled primarily through general powers given to the police to 'maintain order'. The use of surveillance in policing demonstrations is something of a grey area in terms of regulation; although the type of surveillance used does not necessarily target specific individuals, the Security Services Act 1996[3] and the Police Act 1997[4] state that concerted action by many people, even if in itself not illegal, may be investigated as 'serious crime'.

The Anti-Terrorism, Crime and Security Act 2001[5] strengthens the powers of the state to hold traffic data. It also allows government departments to pool their information on terrorism and serious crime as part of their investigations.

Controls over the monitoring of communications data are less restrictive than those for directed surveillance. Communications data are accessible to local government agencies as well as the police or security services.

The Regulation of Investigatory Powers (RIP) Act widened the scope of powers for surveillance. It introduced a new requirement for telecommunications service providers to install special taps to facilitate blanket surveillance based around the automated collection of traffic data.

The RIP Act provides that communications data may be intercepted:

■ in the interests of public safety;

■ for the protection of public health;

■ for the collection of tax or charges payable to a government department; or

■ for preventing death or injury.

It requires that message contents, on the other hand, should only be read in cases involving:

■ national security;

■ the prevention of serious crime;

■ the protection of the 'economic well-being' of the UK.

The European Cybercrime Convention[6] permits communications data to be routinely databased and held for many years and shared with other states that are signatories to the Convention.[7]

Safeguards for the rights of individuals in terms of the use of their personal data come under data protection laws. The rights of individuals to privacy are defined by the Human Rights Act 1998, which implements the European Convention on Human Rights. Article 8 of the Convention states that:

■ Everyone has the right to respect for his/her private and family life, his/her home and his/her correspondence.

■ There shall be no interference by a public authority with the exercise of this right except such as is in accordance with the law and is necessary in a democratic society in the interests of national security, public safety or the economic well-being of the country, for the prevention of disorder or crime, for the protection of health or morals, or for the protection of the rights and freedoms of others.

Under UK law, therefore, a person has no absolute privacy rights. They are all subject to the

Internet and e-mail privacy

Which of the following organisations should have access to internet and telephone records without first seeking authority from the courts

Intelligence services e.g. MI5	65%
Police	63%
Government department	59%
Quangos	22%
Local councils	19%
None of them	21%
Don't know	1%

I am worried about the security of my personal information travelling on the internet and email

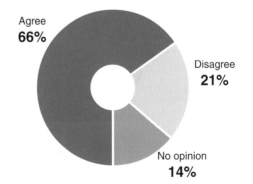

Agree **66%**

Disagree **21%**

No opinion **14%**

ICM Research interviewed a random selection of 1002 adults aged 18+ by telephone between 12-14 July. Interviews were conducted across the country and the results have been weighted to the profile of all adults. *Source: Guardian Newspapers Limited 2003*

exceptions above, so there is a wide range of circumstances in which government and other bodies may argue for such exceptions to be made.

Does the use of electronic surveillance threaten civil liberties?

In situations where data has been used (even where information is erroneous) in a way that damages a person's private life, individuals have limited legal rights to prevent further disclosure or to seek redress for the damage caused.

Many internet privacy activists believe that there may be significant cause for concern on the privacy implications in the use of, for example:
- data profiling;
- the growing number of software tools that can only be registered online;
- internet firewalls and cookies;
- communications traffic data which identify the source of

requests, names of files supplied, dates, times, etc. This can enable the generation of profiles of the activities of groups or individuals;
- the databasing and archiving of that information.

References

1   Regulation of Investigatory Powers Act 2000 – www.legislation. hmso.gov.uk/acts/acts2000/ 20000023.htm
2   Terrorism Act 2000 – www.legislation.hmso.gov.uk/acts/ acts2000/20000011.htm
3   Section 2, Security Services Act 1996 – www.legislation. hmso.gov.uk/acts/acts1996/ 1996035.htm
4   Section 93, Police Act 1997 – www.legislation.hmso.gov.uk/acts/ acts1997/1997050.htm
5   Anti-Terrorism, Crime and Security Act 2001 – www.legislation. hmso.gov.uk/acts/acts2001/ 20010024.htm
6   Council of Europe Cybercrime Convention – conventions.coe.int/ treaty/en/projects/ FinalCybercrime.htm
7   See also GreenNet CSIR Toolkit Briefing no. 8 on Cybercrime.

■ The above information is from GreenNet Educational Trust's internet rights web site which can be found at www.internetrights.org.uk

The Civil Society Internet Rights Project (CSIR) is a GreenNet Educational Trust (GET)-sponsored initiative to provide knowledge, resources and tools for civil society organisations to safely and productively use the Internet as a means of increasing democracy and to campaign on social justice issues.

These materials are produced in cooperation with Paul Mobbs and are licensed under a Creative Commons Attribution-NonCommercial-ShareAlike License.

© GreenNet Educational Trust (GET)

Eyes on the child

The Soham murder trial highlighted the use of mobile phone tracking. But how effective is the technology for consumers, asks S.A. Mathieson

Mobile phone tracking has become one of the hottest new mobile applications. Several services now allow users to track the location of mobile phones, with many making concerned parents their key market.

Many of the service's new customers will undoubtedly have been persuaded to sign up because of the Soham murder trial. A vital piece of prosecution evidence was provided by mobile phone records that pinpointed the location of Holly Wells and Jessica Chapman outside the home of murderer Ian Huntley.

But despite such high-profile successes, there are question marks over the accuracy and security of the data provided to users. The location information comes from the mobile operators and, specifically, relies on which base station a phone is using to connect to its network.

For a switched-on mobile phone, whose owner has given permission, the networks will provide location data with up-to-the-minute accuracy – for a price. You will be able to see the precise location of the base station they are using, and a circle of accuracy within which the network believes the phone to be located. If the person being tracked uses the Vodafone

network, you can even retrieve the last base station used by a switched-off phone, and the time of disconnection.

The problem is that base stations are sited to provide the best coverage, not to track the location of users. The circle of accuracy can have a diameter of a few hundred yards in a city centre, but several miles elsewhere. Vodafone and O2 use base stations with a maximum range of 35km (22 miles), and Orange and T-Mobile stations (the network used by Virgin Mobile) have a 17km range.

However, the geography of an area can cause strange readings. Richard Cox, a forensic expert in the field of mobile phone location, says he has seen a phone in Weston-super-Mare connect to a base station in Penarth, just south of Cardiff, despite much closer stations in north

Somerset. 'Anywhere with two coasts, or a valley, could do this,' he says.

Online found this effect when testing such a service using an Orange mobile phone. In the readings provided, the phone was within the circle of accuracy – but it was sometimes a rather large circle.

A test from Saltash, a sizeable town in Cornwall, showed the phone connecting through a base station in St Budeaux in west Plymouth, almost twice as far away as an Orange base on the Saltash side of the Tamar Bridge. However, there is a clear line of sight from the test location to that part of Plymouth. The resulting accuracy circle was 4.6 miles in diameter, which includes not only Saltash, but also half of Plymouth and the Cornish town of Torpoint.

The size of the accuracy circle is generated by the signal strength, which allows an estimate of the user's distance from the base station. But it is not that accurate, and as a result one cannot say where the tracked phone is in circle. Despite the accuracy circle's radius of 2.3 miles, the phone in Saltash was just 1.1 miles from the Plymouth station. A separate test in north Somerset, with a phone 1.3 miles from the base station, also produced a 2.3-mile-radius circle.

The service tested was Mapaphone by Mapbyte, although all use the same data from the phone networks. Mapaphone only works on Windows PCs running Internet Explorer with Java Virtual Machine, and costs £10 a year for each mobile tracked, a £2.95 monthly subscription fee (which also provides access to mapping and information services) and 20p each time a location is requested.

Its rival ChildLocate charges £9.99 a month, but this includes up to eight mobiles and up to 10 location requests. Further requests cost 30p each.

Mobile phones will eventually include GPS technology. But even releasing middling-quality location data raises privacy questions

---

'Cell ID tracking isn't very accurate,' says Emma Hardcastle, managing director of Mapbyte. She says the service is aimed mainly at companies wanting to see when their vehicles will arrive, rather than parents. For the latter, she says that satellite-based global positioning system (GPS) products are more suitable, as they are accurate to within a few yards.

And the data available from base station services are nothing like as good as those available to police and other government investigators.

Mobile phones will eventually include GPS technology. But even releasing middling-quality location data raises privacy questions.

Mapbyte requires parents wanting to track their children, and employers tracking staff, to sign a form. In the case of children, the parent is then emailed a Pin, which they must enter into the child's phone, to prevent strangers activating the service.

Mapbyte sends tracked mobiles reminder text messages, 24 hours after tracking starts then every month, stating who is tracking the phone and explaining how to opt out. ChildLocate sends such reminders every fortnight.

Privacy campaigner Spy.org.uk has questioned the security of these services, pointing out that several do not use encryption (although Mapbyte and ChildLocate do). The group also raises questions about the service providers' staff, suggesting they should go through criminal record checks.

Finally, there's the question of whether parents should track their children. Terri Dowty, policy director of Action on Rights for Children, says: 'I think this is a very destructive idea – a really cynical exploitation of parents' fears. We all have to face letting our children go and trusting them. You can't keep them on a lead for ever.'

© *Guardian Newspapers Limited 2004*

When knowledge is power

The Data Protection Act can help you fight red tape, says Andrew Bibby

What do you do if you can't get a loan because, let's say, a credit reference company has mixed up your personal details with those of somebody living many streets away?

This was exactly the difficulty facing Paul Ticher and his partner Gill Taylor when they decided to remortgage with the Nationwide. Major credit reference company Experian had amalgamated their file with that of a complete stranger, also with the surname Taylor, who lived in a street with a similar name – but hundreds of yards away and with a totally different postcode. It meant that Nationwide was unable to release the funds, and this in turn cost Paul and Gill more than £150 in extra payments on their old mortgage.

Faced with the prospect of long and protracted correspondence with Experian, Ticher, a consultant and trainer on data protection issues for voluntary organisations, knew he had another route open to him. He used his rights under the Data Protection Act's Assessment procedures to ask the Information Commissioner to rule whether Experian was in breach of its legal data protection obligations.

Three weeks later, the Information Commissioner's assessment came back, confirming Paul's view: Experian had indeed failed to comply with two data protection principles, requiring data to be accurate and relevant.

'Armed with that, I asked Experian to reimburse the money I had overpaid on my mortgage plus some money for associated distress,' Ticher says. Experian corrected the mistakes on the credit files and, even better, a cheque for £300 came from the company a few weeks later.

The Data Protection Act brought into UK law potentially powerful safeguards for personal data agreed at European level, but its operation remains a mystery to most people. Ticher believes the assessment process should be better known.

> *The Data Protection Act brought into UK law potentially powerful safeguards for personal data agreed at European level, but its operation remains a mystery to most people*

'It could be valuable in lots of cases – look at all the utility companies that are messing up people's accounts, for example,' he says. 'Anyone who's lost money from inaccurate data could have a claim for compensation.'

He is not alone in making use of the Act. Antoinette Carter parked briefly in an empty private car park in Notting Hill Gate one Sunday afternoon to drop clothes off in a nearby charity shop. When she returned she found the car clamped. 'When the security guard came to relieve me of the £100 clamp fee, he said he'd seen me on the CCTV monitor,' she says.

She paid up, but as data protection officer for the British Council, she also knew what to do next. 'They had no CCTV sign anywhere. I wrote to the company, said that this amounted to unlawful processing, and received a refund in the post a few weeks later.'

Charles Oppenheim, professor of information science at Loughborough University, has an even

How to get your own back

Adapt a letter like this to your circumstances:

Data Protection Manager,
The Too Big Corporation,
London.

Dear Sir/Madam,
I have today received a letter from your organisation (ref XXXXX), threatening court action for an unpaid bill of £500.

I have already advised your organisation on several occasions, most recently in my letter of 1 October, that you are confusing me with another person with a similar name.

It is my opinion that you are clearly in breach of data protection principles 3 (data must be adequate, relevant and not excessive) and 4 (data must be accurate). Unless I have an adequate response from you within 14 days, I intend to contact the Information Commissioner and ask formally for an assessment to be carried out, under section 42 of the Data Protection Act 1998.

I have also suffered direct financial loss and associated distress as a result of your mistake, and I reserve the right in due course to discuss compensation with you for this, as provided for under the terms of the Data Protection Act.

Yours faithfully

better story to tell. He has successfully used the Data Protection Act no less than three times to sort out bureaucratic bungling, including the occasion when the loss of his old mortgage records by Abbey National threatened to jeopardise his right to a £20,000 endowment-policy payout.

'I wrote to the data protection manager at Abbey National and said "You're in breach of the Act",' he says. 'It's a very powerful weapon against large organisations, which can act like juggernauts. It needs a lot more publicity.'

The challenging task of upholding the law and promoting compliance with the eight official data-processing principles takes place in an office block in Wilmslow, Cheshire, where the Information Commissioner is based. By general consensus hopelessly under-resourced for the task it faces, this public agency tries to achieve results by persuasion and pressure rather than by sanction. It has no power to award compensation for individuals who have suffered loss. Nevertheless, the Act requires the Commissioner to make formal assessments on request from individuals who believe that data protection principles, such as data accuracy or relevance, have been breached.

'We're trying to ensure that there's good public awareness of this,' says Jonathan Bamford, assistant commissioner at the agency. He says that requests for assessment are more likely to be dealt with quickly if individuals can show that they have already tried to get companies to sort out problems and errors.

He also points out that there is a right under the Act to claim compensation through the courts if people can demonstrate they have suffered damage and distress.

'The good thing about the right to assessment is that, by making a judgment, we're giving people a mechanism for them to show to the court – for them to say "I suffered loss, therefore please award me compensation",' he says.

However, very few people appear to be using this facility. Last year, the Information Commissioner dealt with only 12,000 assessments, a figure which also includes initial public inquiries falling outside the provisions of the Act.

Perhaps significantly, 20% of these assessments and inquiries concerned credit reference files, an area to which the Information Commissioner is devoting considerable resources.

As Ticher's case demonstrates, invoking the assessment procedure can resolve problems without the need for court action. 'I'm really pleased with the way the system worked.

'The mechanism did seem to be there, even if it is slightly creaky, to get things sorted out,' he says.

■ This article first appeared in *The Observer*, 16 November 2003.

New 'snooper's charter' faces legal challenge

By Philip Johnston, Home Affairs Editor

The so-called 'snooper's charter', which will allow public agencies to gather data about telephone and email traffic, could be illegal, according to privacy campaigners.

New regulations will give more than 24 state bodies and hundreds of local government officials the power to demand personal communications details, though not the content, of messages and calls.

Organisations ranging from the Environment Agency and the Information Commission to the Gaming Board and Food Standards Agency will be able to obtain the information.

Others with the powers include NHS trusts, the Financial Services Authority, the Royal Mail and more than 450 local authorities.

The Government says the agencies need the data to enforce the law. The data can include names and addresses of customers, their service use records, details of who has called whom, mobile phone locations and the sources and destinations of emails.

But Privacy International said a legal opinion from Covington and Burling, an international law firm, suggested the new regulations were unlawful under the European Convention of Human Rights. 'Article 8 guarantees every individual the right to respect for his or her private life, subject only to narrow exceptions where government action is imperative,' the firm said.

'The indiscriminate collection of traffic data offends a core principle of the rule of law: that citizens should have notice of the circumstances in which the state may conduct surveillance, so that they can regulate their behaviour to avoid unwanted intrusions.'

The firm says that an EU directive on data retention, which 10 countries have adopted, also falls foul of human rights laws.

'Under the case law of the European Court of Human Rights, such a disproportionate interference in the private lives of individuals cannot be said to be necessary in a democratic society,' it adds.

Simon Davies, a director of Privacy International, said it would pursue test cases in at least two EU countries where there was mandatory retention.

'This is an important legal analysis,' he said. 'It clearly exposes the Government's intention to snoop unnecessarily on innocent people.

'The Government's plans are illegal. We are calling on all communications providers to support their customers' rights by ignoring the Government's proposals.'

The 'snoopers' charter' explained

The Home Office has published a consultation paper detailing who it thinks should have access to private data and for how long. Neil McIntosh explains what's behind the so-called snoopers' charter

What is the snoopers' charter?

It's a plan to give state agencies access to your telephone, internet and email records. Data would include information including whom you call on your mobile phone, and where you are calling from, and to whom and when you sent emails.

I've read 'Spycatcher' – didn't they have access already?

Some agencies – the police, MI5 and MI6, the government listening post GCHQ, the Inland Revenue and Customs and Excise – already had access. But the new proposals extend the number of agencies that can access these communications data.

Who will be able to find out what I'm up to?

The revised plans announced 11 March 2003 extend the automatic power to see this information to agencies with crime-fighting roles, like the UK Atomic Energy Constabulary, the Scottish Drugs Enforcement Agency and the Maritime and Coastguard Agency. Fire authorities and NHS trusts will also get full access, so they can investigate suspicious fires and hoax 999 calls. A long list of other organisations, including 468 local councils, the Royal Mail, Food Standards Agency and others, will have more limited powers to access details of phone and internet subscribers.

So why was there such a fuss?

Some campaigners feel such information should remain confidential for all but the most pressing investigations. And early versions of the proposals, which were revealed by the *Guardian* in June last year, sparked an outcry. It was revealed that hundreds of bodies – including your local council, any government department and the NHS – would

By Neil McIntosh

be able to demand full details of your communications without so much as a court order.

What did the privacy campaigners say about that?

At the time Simon Davies, director of Privacy International, called the plans 'a systematic attack on the right to privacy'. John Wadham, director of Liberty, said the list demonstrated 'it is not just the police who will be looking at our communications records. It is practically every public servant who will be able to play this game.'

So then it became law, right?

Wrong. In a move that surprised everyone, David Blunkett backed down, admitting the government had 'blundered' into its plans. He promised to go away and think again, and consult his son Hugh, 24, who works in IT.

And that's where the new plans have come from?

Correct (from the consultation, that is – Hugh's exact involvement is unclear). Yesterday the home secretary said he took concerns about intrusion into privacy 'very seriously'. He added: 'To succeed in allaying fears of a Big Brother approach . . . government needs to secure public confidence that the boundary between privacy and protecting the public is set correctly.'

And the privacy campaigners – are they happy?

They are a little happier than last summer, but still warn of trouble ahead. Simon Davies warned he thought the plans were a 'Trojan horse' to 'open up the entire debate about privacy'. John Wadham said he welcomed much of the new plan – but said there was still a need for safeguards, including judicial scrutiny of requests for data.

© Guardian Newspapers Limited 2004

CCTV and human rights

By Rachel Armitage

Data Protection Act 1998 and Human Rights Act 1998

Under the Data Protection Act 1998, CCTV systems that process data must be notified to the Information Commissioner (formerly the Data Protection Commissioner). Systems installed from 1 March 2000 must be automatically registered; those installed before 24 October 1998 should have been registered by 2001. When registering a system, the user must state what the purpose of the system is. Once registered compliance with a number of legally enforceable principles is required. The Data Protection Act requires that information be obtained fairly and lawfully, this includes codes of practice such as:

- Appropriately sized signs (A4 or A3) must be displayed where CCTV is in place.
- Signs should display a 'purpose of the system message'.
- The data/images captured should be used for the original purpose intended for the scheme.
- Cameras should be positioned to ensure that they avoid capturing images that are irrelevant or intrusive.
- Individuals have a right to a copy of any personal data held about them.[1]

Public authorities such as the police, local authorities, prisons, government departments and courts are also bound by Article 8 of the Human Rights Act 1998 which came into force in October 2000. Article 8 states that:

- Everyone has the right to respect for his private and family life, his home and his correspondence.
- There shall be no interference by a public authority with the exercise of this right except such as is in accordance with the law and is necessary in a democratic society in the interests of national security, public safety or the economic wellbeing of the country, for the prevention of

nacro

**changing lives
reducing crime**

disorder or crime, for the protection of health or morals, or for the protection of the rights or freedoms of others.

In order to comply with Article 8, public authorities should consider the following principles:[2]

CCTV *users must ensure that their monitoring practices are governed by the Codes of Practice and Procedures*

Proportionality
Does the level of threat or risk to community safety warrant the existence of a CCTV scheme? Is the level of coverage commensurate to the level of crime and disorder? Is there a balance between public safety and the rights of the individual?

Legality
CCTV operators must be fully aware and signed up to the system Codes of Practice and Procedures. All actions must be supported by legislation or

stated cases, this legislation may include: Section 17 of the Crime and Disorder Act 1998, Section 6 of the Police Act 1967, Section 163 of the Criminal Justice and Public Order Act 1994, and Section 3 of the Criminal Law Act 1967.

Accountability
CCTV users must ensure that their monitoring practices are governed by the Codes of Practice and Procedures.

Necessity/compulsion
Is the surveillance necessary at all? Are there other crime reduction measures which would achieve the same ends?

Subsidiarity
The operation of the CCTV system should cause minimum interference with the privacy of the individual.

Although complying with such regulations avoids litigation, these guidelines are also designed to ensure that CCTV systems can be used to their maximum effect. As is highlighted in the advertising campaign from the Metropolitan Police's Anti-Terrorist Branch, unless cameras are set up and maintained correctly they are very little use.

References
1 For more information, including a Checklist of Operating Procedures, see the Home Office Crime Reduction web site (www.crime reduction.gov.uk/cctv9.htm and www.crimereduction.gov.uk/cctv24b.pdf).
2 Adapted from the Home Office Crime Reduction web site (www.crimereduction.gov.uk/cctv13.htm).

- The above information is an extract from a Nacro briefing entitled *To CCTV or not to CCTV?* For more information visit their web site which can be found at www.nacro.org.uk
© *Nacro*

Beware secret cameras in the loo

Employers are resorting to controversial methods to spy on staff. But how far does the law allow workers' privacy rights to be infringed?

By Clare Dyer

What's the sneakiest and most privacy-invading trick you can imagine an employer playing on an unsuspecting worker? Reading your emails on the quiet? Listening in on your private phone calls? Planting a hidden CCTV camera behind your desk? Step forward, Warwick University, and claim your title as intrusive employer of the year.

With the headlines full of sackings for sending dodgy emails or downloading porn, most of us have probably twigged that the computers we use at work are far from private. But few would expect an employer's surveillance to extend into our kitchens or living rooms.

To be fair, the trick wasn't played by the university itself, but was perpetrated in its name by its insurers, who were defending a former worker's accident claim. Insurers normally take over the full running of any claims covered by their insurance; in this case the university says it was unaware of their modus operandi and indeed was surprised the case was still running after six years. But the tale of Jean Jones raises serious questions about how far the law allows a worker's privacy rights to be infringed.

Jones, 65, was working in the student shop at Warwick in 1997 when a full cash box with a broken lid fell on her right wrist, inflicting a small cut between the fourth and fifth fingers of her hand. In her legal action against the university, which has not yet reached trial, she claimed around £135,000 in special damages, mainly loss of earnings, because of continuing disability in her hand. The insurers argue that she had virtually recovered five years ago. Their medical expert says her

> *With the headlines full of sackings for sending dodgy emails or downloading porn, most of us have probably twigged that the computers we use at work are far from private*

ongoing disability 'remains uncertain but it seems to be more related to habit than need'.

In late 1999 and early 2000, Jones twice invited into her home a woman who turned up on her doorstep claiming to be a market researcher. What she didn't know was that her visitor was an inquiry agent hired by the university's insurers. She secretly videotaped Jones to see if her hand was really as bad as she claimed. The insurers' medical experts say the tape shows her hand functioning perfectly well; her experts claim her condition is variable, with good and bad days.

The insurers' ploy came into the public domain only because they had to go to court to try to win the right to use the film in evidence. Jones' lawyers cited the European convention on human rights, part of UK law since October 2000, which guarantees respect for an individual's private life. Last month the insurers were strongly criticised by the court of appeal for behaviour which was both an invasion of privacy and, as a trespass, illegal. It was 'improper and not justified', said the lord chief justice, Lord Woolf. The insurers' motivation to achieve a just result

'does not justify either the commission of trespass or the contravention of the claimant's privacy which took place'.

But while the judges acknowledged that the inquiry agent had gained improper access to Jones' home and penalised the insurers by ordering them to pay costs, they still gave the go-ahead for the videotape to be used in evidence. Lord Woolf said it would be 'artificial and undesirable' for the tape not to be put before the judge who will eventually try the case.

He made the ruling while conceding: 'There will be cases in which a claimant's privacy will be infringed and the evidence obtained will confirm that the claimant has not exaggerated the claim in any way. This could still be the result in this case.'

The appeal court's censure may make other insurance companies think twice before including the sham market researcher as the latest tool in their armoury. But you don't have to be suing your employers to be snooped on at their behest. Venture outdoors when you are off sick and your every move could be noted down and used against you.

The prison service hired a husband-and-wife team of private eyes to watch an executive officer who was off work with depression. Managers suspected that she might be working in the dress shop she owned. The detectives saw her open the shop on two days but failed to disclose the four days of surveillance in which they saw nothing. She was sacked for gross misconduct but later won a claim for unfair dismissal.

So did a maintenance engineer with 17 years' experience who was videotaped going to the doctor and the chemist and taking his son to school during a week when he was off sick. The tribunal held that sacking him was unfair and awarded him compensation.

There is even more chance that Big Brother is watching you while you are at your desk. As email increasingly replaces the telephone, employers fear that smutty messages sent by employees could land them with sexual harassment claims or could besmirch their reputation.

Technology now allows emails to be monitored for dubious content and porn downloads identified.

Does your employer need your consent to monitor your emails, calls and internet access? Not if the purpose of the exercise is to monitor business communications. This covers interception for a wide range of purposes, including establishing the existence of facts – such as advice given to customers – or the standards workers are achieving; to prevent or detect crime; to detect unauthorised use of the IT system; or to check for viruses or other threats to the system.

Does your employer need your consent to monitor your emails, calls and internet access? Not if the purpose of the exercise is to monitor business communications

---

Interception without consent is allowed if the purpose is to check whether communications are business-related or not. This would allow the emails of an employee who was away to be opened to check whether action was needed (though it would not allow any emails marked 'personal' in the header to be read). And no consent is needed for interceptions carried out only for the purpose of gaining access to the contents of business emails, but which 'may incidentally and unavoidably involve some access to other communications'.

Even if your internet traffic isn't monitored, your downloads could still betray you, as the manager of a

legal practice discovered recently when he lost his £60,000-a-year job. The company which supplied the IT system was called in after the computers kept crashing, and an investigation showed that the manager had been spending up to four hours a day tucked away in his office accessing porn sites. Not only was he being paid full-time for working half-time, but the practice was being charged at high rates for the porn he was downloading.

In 2000 the former information commissioner Elizabeth France drew up a code of practice to regulate workplace monitoring of emails and internet use, CCTV and covert surveillance. Three years later, after much toing and froing with unions and employers' representatives – who inevitably don't see eye to eye on how much privacy employees should have – the code is still in draft. In January the TUC called on the new information commissioner Richard Thomas to 'resist employer lobbying' and introduce the code. It pointed out that the Data Protection Act had come into force in October 2001 but employers still had no guide as to how to exercise their legal responsibilities and protect employees' privacy.

The draft code says employers should usually tell employees if their emails and internet use are being automatically intercepted, and why. Ditto if the workplace is monitored by CCTV cameras. Covert monitoring of employees by CCTV is rarely justified, says the code. Employers should use it only where there are grounds to suspect criminal activities are taking place and notifying workers about the monitoring would prejudice an investigation.

Hidden cameras should not usually be used in places where workers would expect privacy, such as toilets or individual offices. The code adds, however, that they could be justified even in toilets, if for instance there was evidence of drug dealing on the premises, though monitoring in such a case would normally be under the control of the police. So there is no guarantee of privacy at work – not even in the loo.

© *Guardian Newspapers Limited 2004*

Someone to watch over the office police

A new code on monitoring aims to balance an employee's right to privacy with a company's interests

By Michael Becket

Employers should monitor workers only after telling them why and how it is to be done, according to a new code of practice from the Information Commissioner, Richard Thomas.

He said 'monitoring in the workplace can be intrusive, whether examining emails, recording phone calls or installing CCTV cameras. Employees are entitled to expect that their personal lives remain private and they have a degree of privacy in the work environment.'

The overall aim is to strike a balance between a worker's legitimate right to respect for their private life and an employer's legitimate need to run a business, he added.

The code recommends a comprehensive assessment to see if the company really does have to monitor at all. That includes checking the benefits against the effect on employees, and seeing how the same benefits could be achieved through some less intrusive method. A specific impact assessment for each type of monitoring should check if it is relevant, appropriate and complies with the law.

The Data Protection Act can prompt criminal prosecutions and other sanctions against directors, and employees unlawfully monitored can claim damages. Mr Thomas added 'only in exceptional circumstances will it be appropriate for employers to monitor their employees without their knowledge', such as for detecting or preventing crime.

David Smith, deputy commissioner, explained that covert surveillance was also permissible for some equivalent problems such as suspected selling of a company's trade secrets to a competitor. The code does not impose new legal obligations and it contains a short guidance section for small business, though their data protection responsibilities when monitoring are the same as for major corporations, Mr Smith said.

Mark Mansell of Allen & Overy said the code is 'significantly better than employers had feared. The first draft had made it almost impossible to monitor' but the latest version should present no problems for companies so long as they act sensibly. It provides a sensible balance between the needs of the employer but 'gives employees some feeling of security that their privacy will be observed', Mr Mansell added.

> *'Employees are entitled to expect that their personal lives remain private and they have a degree of privacy in the work environment'*

The code does not actually define monitoring but explains it does include CCTV cameras, opening emails or voicemails, checking internet usage, automated checking software, listening to or keeping records of telephone calls, gathering information from point of sale terminals, or checking with credit reference agencies.

This is the latest of a series of four codes which are not themselves law, but courts will take them into account in data privacy cases. Simeon Spencer of Morrison & Foerster said: 'A well-informed and properly prepared employer should not have any real concerns on either the code or the Data Protection Act.'

He warned however that 'wider employment rights may also be affected and may result in claims against the employer, for example, for unfair dismissal. Staff need to understand why they are being monitored and how the information gleaned from monitoring will be used.

'Work-time lost through unauthorised net surfing and wider liabilities created by employees misusing computers are legitimate concerns for any employer,' said Mr Spencer.

Disciplinary proceedings for email and internet abuse at work in the previous 12 months exceeded those for dishonesty, violence and health and safety breaches put together, according to a survey last autumn by KLegal and *Personnel Today* magazine.

Sending pornographic emails was one of the three most common causes for sacking staff – nearly 40pc of disciplinary cases resulted in dismissal. By comparison almost all the staff who were found to be dishonest were sacked, and 74pc of the employees disciplined for violence were dismissed. Nearly two-thirds of email and internet-related dismissals were for accessing or distributing pornographic material.

The law firm associated with KPMG added it is becoming increasingly important for businesses to get their policies on employee usage right. Companies are monitoring their workers' internet usage more than they used to, but nearly 10pc were breaking the law by not telling the workers.

Sending pornographic emails was one of the three most common causes for sacking staff – nearly 40pc of disciplinary cases resulted in dismissal

---

Tim Johnson, of KLegal, said the new code may well increase the regulatory burden on businesses, but it is there to balance between the company's interests and the employee's right to privacy. The Information Commissioner's codes on job applications and pre-employment vetting, and employment records have already been published.

The final code, on health, medical testing, drug and genetic screening, had a consultation two years ago but everybody became so preoccupied with the monitoring code that it got little attention. Mr Smith said another round of consultation would be sensible to make sure the results are up to date, but the aim is still to have the code in place by the end of the year.

The codes have not been published in a single volume because of their length.

© *Telegraph Group Limited, London 2004*

Workplace privacy

Time for European-level workplace privacy regulation

The use of new information and communication technologies (ICT) at the workplace has spread rapidly in recent years. This raises numerous issues for employers, employees and their representatives, especially in terms of the relationship between workers' privacy and employers' need to control and monitor the use of ICT.

The August 2003 comparative study from the European Industrial Relations Observatory (EIRO) focuses on an important issue resulting from the growth of ICT: the relationship between internet/email use at work and respect for workers' privacy. It highlights the need for clear regulation at European level by mapping and comparing the differences in existing European and national law on workplace privacy, and it offers the views of the social partners. The matter is especially topical at present, with the European Commission expected to propose a Directive on workplace data protection in 2004 or 2005.

While the Charter of Fundamental Rights of the European Union and other national data protection legislation clearly spell out the privacy rights of the individual, the rules and regulations governing privacy at the workplace are based on a complex web of guidelines and individual agreements at company level, often compromising either the individual worker's or the employer's rights.

Against the backdrop of increasing use of new technology, and particularly of email and the internet in the employment context, the frontier between private life and work life is becoming increasingly blurred. The EIRO study concludes that the use of new technology at the workplace must be examined as part of a broader context incorporating respect for privacy and the protection of personal data in a work setting.

Against the backdrop of increasing use of new technology, the frontier between private life and work life is becoming increasingly blurred

---

The risks of conflicting interests on either side of the employment relationship have grown sharply over the last few years, given the increased use of ICT at the workplace and in all aspects of enterprises' activities. The EIRO study asks such pertinent questions as: 'To what extent may a worker use ICT equipment for private reasons given that a general ban on the use of the internet for other than professional reasons does not appear realistic in an information communication society?' and 'How far can employers' actions aimed at preventing potential dangers be extended without undermining workers' fundamental rights?'

■ The EIRO comparative study, *New technology and the respect for privacy at the workplace*, is available at www.eiro.eurofound.eu.int/2003/07/study/TN0307101S.html

■ The above information is from the European Foundation for the Improvement of Living and Working Condition's web site which can be found at www.eurofound.eu.int

© *European Foundation for the Improvement of Living and Working Conditions*

Monitoring and internet policies

Information from workSMART from the TUC

What is monitoring at work?

Monitoring is to some extent a routine part of the employer/employee relationship. Most employers make some checks on the quantity and quality of work produced by their staff, and employees will generally expect this.

Some employers carry out monitoring to safeguard workers, as well as to protect their own interests or those of their customers. For example, monitoring may help ensure that workers in hazardous jobs aren't at risk from unsafe working practices, or in some financial services, employers have legal or regulatory obligations, which they can only fulfil by using some monitoring.

However, where monitoring goes beyond just watching the performance of an individual, and involves the collection, processing and storage of personal data, it needs to be done in a way that is both lawful and fair to staff.

For more information on this, and a helpful guide for employers, you can visit the website of the Government Information Commissioner which can be found at www.informationcommissioner.gov.uk

How should my employer approach monitoring at work?

If used in inappropriate ways or in the wrong situations, monitoring can have an adverse impact on staff. It can intrude into their private lives, disrupt their work, or interfere with the relationship of mutual trust and confidence between them and their employer.

If there would be any adverse impact on workers, the Data Protection Act requires it to be justified by the benefits that the employer and others would gain from the monitoring.

The Information Commissioner has set out guidance for employers in

workSMART
FROM THE TUC

the Employment Practice Data Protection Code. This Code draws together the obligations on employers in the Data Protection Act, the Human Rights Act 1998, the Regulation of Investigatory Powers Act 2000 (RIPA), and the influence of the EC Directive 95/46/EC. Whilst the Code is not a legal obligation in itself, it is formulated to comply with legal obligations, so if your employer is not adhering to the Code, they may be breaking one or more of the laws which it is based on.

The Code of Practice suggests that in all but the most minor cases, employers carry out an 'impact assessment' in deciding if and how to use monitoring. This involves measuring the benefits monitoring will bring, any adverse impact on workers, whether comparable benefits can be obtained with a lesser impact, and the techniques available for carrying out monitoring. They must decide whether the monitoring is a proportionate response to the problem it seeks to address. An impact assessment should:

- clearly identify the purpose behind the monitoring arrangement, and the benefits it is likely to deliver
- identify any likely adverse impact of the monitoring arrangement on staff, including their private lives within the workplace
- consider alternatives to monitoring, or different ways in which it might be carried out with less disruption
- take into account the obligations that arise from monitoring

- judge whether monitoring is justified, considering the above factors and results of any consultation with unions or other staff representatives.

Am I being monitored without my knowledge?

It is a general requirement of the Data Protection Act that where the carrying out of monitoring results in the collection or other processing of personal data, those who are subject to it should be made aware that it is being carried out and why it is being carried out.

Where video or audio monitoring takes place, staff should have specific information such as the location of cameras or microphones. Where communications are monitored the information may be less specific but staff should know when to expect that information about them will be collected.

The Information Commissioner's Code of Practice on monitoring suggests that employers make this information available in staff handbooks, intranets, or other places where staff usually find out about personnel policy, and that staff are updated if significant changes are introduced.

The only exception to this principle of notifying staff is where an employer is justified in using covert monitoring to investigate a genuine suspicion of criminal activity or serious wrongdoing.

Do I need to give consent for my employer to monitor me at work?

Employers who can justify monitoring on the basis of a properly conducted impact assessment do not generally need the consent of individual workers.

Indeed, even if workers do freely give their consent, the employer should still conduct an objective impact assessment.

Consent is only likely to be relevant where an employer sets out to collect sensitive data through monitoring.

What counts as personal information for the purposes of monitoring at work?

Personal information is information which relates to a living person, and identifies an individual, whether by itself, or together with other information.

All computerised personal datapersonal information is covered by the Data Protection Act. It also covers personal information on paper or microfiche and held in any 'relevant filing system', as is information recorded with the intention that it will be filed or computerised. A 'relevant filing system' essentially means any set of information about workers in which it is easy to find a piece of information about a particular individual.

Examples of personal information include:
- details of a worker's salary and bank account held on an organisation's computer system or in a manual filing system
- an e-mail about an incident involving a named worker
- a supervisor's notebook containing sections on several named workers
- a set of completed application forms.

There are additional regulations in the Data Protection Act governing 'sensitive data', which is information concerning an individual's:
- racial or ethnic origin
- political opinions
- religious beliefs or other beliefs of a similar nature
- trade union membership
- physical or mental health or condition
- sexual life
- commission or alleged commission of any offence, or proceedings for any offence committed or alleged to have been committed.

The Data Protection Act sets out a series of conditions, at least one of which has to apply before an employer can collect, store, use, disclose or otherwise process sensitive data.

Do I have a right to know what information my employer has collected through monitoring me at work?

The Data Protection Act gives any individual the right to request to see what information has been stored on them by any data processor, and staff are not exempted from this. Your employer should present you with this information on request.

The Information Commissioner's Approved Code of Practice in monitoring also requires employers to share information with workers, if it would have an adverse impact on them, and before taking any action. Automated monitoring results can be incomplete or open to misinterpretation, and staff should be able to see, and if necessary explain or challenge the results of monitoring.

Employers who can justify monitoring on the basis of a properly conducted impact assessment do not generally need the consent of individual workers

---

Personal information collected through monitoring should not be used for purposes other than those for which the monitoring was introduced, unless it is clearly in the individual's interest to do so, or it reveals activity that no employer could reasonably be expected to ignore.

What should be in a good electronic communications policy?

To satisfy data protection requirements, a company's policy for the use of electronic communications should as a minimum:
- set out clearly the circumstances in which employees may or may not use the employer's phone systems (including mobile phones), e-mail system and the internet access for private communications
- make clear the extent and type of private use that is allowed, for example any restrictions on overseas phone calls or limits on the size or type of e-mail attachments
- specify clearly any restrictions on Web material that can be viewed or copied. A simple ban on 'offensive material' is unlikely to be sufficiently clear for workers to know what is and is not allowed. Employers should at least give examples of the sort of material that is considered offensive, e.g. material containing racist terminology or images of nudity
- advise employees what personal information they are allowed to include in particular types of communication, or the alternatives that should be used, e.g. communication with the company doctor should be sent by internal mail rather than e-mail
- lay down clear rules regarding personal use of communication equipment when used from home, e.g. facilities that enable external dialling into a company network
- explain the purposes of any monitoring, its extent, and the means used
- outline how the policy is enforced and the penalties for breaching it.

The existence of an electronic communications policy should also be communicated clearly to staff, and they should be able to access it easily to find out what it covers.

■ The above information is from the TUC's workSMART web site which can be found at www.worksmart.org.uk Alternatively, see page 41 for the TUC's address details.

© TUC

Spam email

Information from the Internet Watch Foundation (IWF)

'Spam' is a general term used to describe Unsolicited Bulk E mails (UBE) usually sent to a large number of email users who have not requested to be contacted by the sender. Spam messages are usually commercial in nature, often containing sales promotions, 'get rich quick' schemes, illegal product information, pornography and occasionally advertising websites containing images of child abuse. But it can also refer to any message that a user receives from a sender whom they have not asked to be contacted by.

Spam is annoying, and it can often be very offensive. It generally comes from people or companies you do not know, who are often trying to sell you something.

Parents should take an interest in what their children do online generally, in particular they should perhaps take an interest in whom they are sending emails to, and who they are receiving them from.

And remember, if you or your child does receive a nasty email, do not immediately think you have been targeted. It's probably spam and therefore indiscriminate.

Almost everyone in the Internet industry wants to stop spam, but it's a lot easier said than done. The great majority of spam comes from overseas, making it exceptionally difficult for the British police or other authorities to do anything directly to apprehend the culprits and put a stop to it.

Tips to help combat spam

- One of the best ways of dealing with spam is simply to delete it! Don't open it, especially if it comes with any kind of attachment. It might contain a virus that could severely damage your computer.
- Be careful whom you give your email address to when you are online. Check out companies' privacy policies before you subscribe to anything or buy anything from them. In Chat Rooms, maybe you should not allow your personal profile to be published and do not disclose your email address. Remember also, if you allow your email address to appear on any web site, it could always be harvested by one of thousands of bots that wander around the Internet looking for them.
- Particularly if you have younger children, think about setting up a list of people they can receive emails from, and send them to. This will block the rest. Several popular email programmes allow you to do this e.g. Outlook Express, under Message Rules. Also ask your Internet Service Provider (ISP) how they can help you.
- The larger, better-known free email service providers seem to attract a huge amount of spam whereas others do not. Check out how effectively different service providers keep spam at bay.

- There are various firewall programmes, anti-spamming software packages and other technical measures that can help keep your email address a secret from various unscrupulous web site owners, or others who harvest people's contact details, or filter your incoming mail. Details of such software and spam in general is available at www.spam.cl.cam.ac.uk/spam
- Another good site for filtering tools is www.getnetwise.org/tools where you will find details of the various types of software, some of which can be downloaded for free. If you click on the 'Tools for Families' icon, you can fill in a questionnaire designed to help identify the most suitable software for your needs.
- Lots of people now have more than one email address: one that they keep relatively private or only give to friends and business associates, and another that they might use if they go surfing or want to sign on for various Internet-based services. That's where the spam will end up.
- On online Forums, Newsgroups or in Chat Rooms consider disguising your email address with 'NOSPAM' or 'REMOVE_ THIS' in the middle to confuse harvesting software but that real people can easily figure out to remove e.g. yournameREMOVE _THIS@yourispname.co.uk vice yourname@yourisp.co.uk
- It is usually best not to respond to any links within an email that give you an opportunity to be removed from the sender's list. A response from you confirms that a 'real person' has been found and may lead to more spam.

- The above information is from the Internet Watch Foundation's web site which can be found at www.iwf.org.uk

Spam offences

Nature of the spam offence and investigation process needs Government clarification

The Internet Services Providers' Association (ISPA UK) has highlighted concerns about the processes used to trace and prosecute spammers and the resources the authorities are willing to commit to such investigations. The views were expressed in ISPA's generally supportive submission to the UK consultation on the Privacy and Electronic Communications Directive, the new European law that regulates bulk unsolicited commercial email and other forms of electronic unsolicited commercial communications.

ISPA would like the Department for Trade and Industry to consider how organisations and individuals breaking the new law will be investigated and the action they will face. The Government should clarify whether the act of disseminating bulk unsolicited commercial communications contrary to the Directive will be a criminal or civil offence. The nature of the offence will determine the type of investigation to be pursued by the authorities and the action to be taken against those who break the law. Furthermore, Government should consider the resource allocation for such investigations.

If the Government determines that sending illegal bulk unsolicited commercial communications is a civil offence then ISPA believes that a clearer framework governing the disclosure of data in relation to the investigation of such offences will be needed. However, if the Government determines that it should be a criminal offence, then the processes set out in the Regulation of Investigatory Powers Act (RIPA) should apply.

Criminal investigations should comply with RIPA

RIPA was introduced to create a single framework to regulate access to communications data by law enforcement agencies for the purpose of criminal investigations only. If it is determined that the sending of illegal electronic unsolicited commercial communications constitutes a criminal offence, ISPA believes that any disclosure of data to assist the investigation should be in line with RIPA requirements and involve the appropriate authorities including the Information Commissioner.

A clearer framework for investigations is needed if sending spam is deemed to be a civil offence

---

ISPA questions whether the authorities will commit sufficient resources to investigate incidents of spam using the RIPA processes.

Investigating civil offences

A clearer framework for investigations is needed if sending spam is deemed to be a civil offence.

ISPA is concerned that without proper and effective regulation, any requirements to disclose source data for purposes connected with the investigation of civil offences could be too far-reaching. The privacy of innocent individuals could be compromised if investigations are conducted on any email sender by claiming they were sending spam.

The need for effective spam laws

Jessica Hendrie-Liaño, Chair of the ISPA Council, said, 'ISPA believes that an effective legal framework is necessary in order to take action against persistent spammers. Such a framework would reinforce the Internet industry's self-regulation and the action already taken by many Internet users to limit spam.'

Privacy and data protection

Have you every done any of the following?

Unlisted your telephone number	37%
Used encryption on emails	13%
Applied under the Data Protection Act to find out what information an organisation holds about you	10%
Used a false name or address when logging on to an internet site to protect your identity	9%
None of these	51%

ICM Research interviewed a random selection of 1002 adults aged 18+ by telephone between 12 and 14 July 2003. Interviews were conducted across the country and the results have been weighted to the profile of all adults.

Source: Guardian Newspapers Limited 2003

She continued, 'ISPA opposes the sending of emails without due regard for applicable law or in contravention of a service provider's terms and conditions. Spam can be irritating, often offensive and is time consuming for recipients to download and work through. Spam saps ISPs' valuable bandwidth, can compromise the integrity of a network and affects the performance of mail servers. Combating spam costs ISPs very significant amounts of time and money.'

ISPA

The Internet Services Providers' Association (ISPA) was established in 1995 as a trade association to represent providers of Internet services in the UK. ISPA promotes competition, self-regulation and the development of the Internet industry. For a list of members or other information about ISPA, please consult the website: http://www.ispa.org.uk

The Privacy and Electronic Communications Directive

The Privacy and Electronic Communications Directive supersedes and updates other laws that relate to electronic unsolicited commercial communications.

The Directive makes the privacy rules that apply to phone and fax services applicable to email and use of the Internet. The Directive sets conditions on the use of traffic, location and subscriber data and regulates the use of communications networks for unsolicited direct marketing by phone, fax, email and SMS.

The Privacy and Electronic Communications Directive clarifies how companies can use mass dissemination of email. Sending bulk unsolicited commercial email (UCE) is prohibited, with limited exceptions. Companies can send UCE to existing customers and selected users that have explicitly consented to receive the information. However the sender must enable the recipients to opt out of any future unsolicited communications.

■ The above information is from the Internet Services Providers' Association's web site which can be found at www.ispa.org.uk

© 2004 – Internet Services Providers' Association, UK.

Communications data protection and retention

Information from GreenNet Educational Trust (GET)

1. What is communications data?

'Communications data' is defined by recent UK laws to include the following:

■ Traffic data – this information identifies who the user contacted, at what time the contact was made, the location of the person contacted and the location of the user;

■ Service data – this information identifies which services were used and for how long;

■ Subscriber data – this information identifies the user of the service, providing their name, address, telephone number.

Communications data does not include the content of any communication.

The person or organisation to whom such data refer is known as the data subject.

The person or organisation holding that data is known as the data controller. Data controllers must be registered with the UK Information Commissioner (an independent supervisory authority which reports directly to Parliament).

2. How is communications data covered by law?

Three UK laws cover data protection and retention. They are:

■ The Data Protection Act 1984
■ The Data Protection Act 1998

■ Anti-Terrorism, Crime and Security Act 2001 (Section II covers data retention)

Section 102 of the above law provides for the Secretary of State to issue a voluntary Code of Practice for communication service providers to retain data. The code is currently under consultation.

The main powers of the 1998 Act came into force on 1 March 2000. Some transitional exemptions are allowed until 24 October 2007, by which time the 1995 European directive must be fully implemented.

The 1998 Act contains eight principles of data protection. Briefly, they are:

1. Processing of personal data must be done fairly and lawfully.
2. Personal data should be obtained only for specified purposes and

must be processed in a manner compatible with those purposes.

3. Personal data must be adequate, relevant, and not excessive in relation to those purposes.

4. Personal data must be accurate and, where necessary, kept up to date.

5. Personal data should not be kept longer than necessary.

6. Personal data must be processed in accordance with the rights of data subjects under the current Data Protection Act.

7. Technical and organisational measures can be taken against unauthorised or unlawful processing of personal data and against accidental loss, destruction or damage to personal data.

8. Personal data should not be transferred outside the European Economic Area unless to a country or territory that ensures an adequate level of protection for the rights and freedoms of data subjects in relation to the processing of personal data.

Personal data is data relating to a living individual who can be identified from reading it, or from a combination of the data and other data held by the data controller. Processing of personal data is covered by Section 2 of the 1998 Act.

Sensitive personal data consists of information on the data subject's:

- racial or ethnic origin;
- political opinions, religious beliefs or similar beliefs;
- membership of a trade union;
- physical or mental health or sexual life;
- criminal offences, or proceedings in relation to alleged offences.

Processing of sensitive personal data is covered by Section 3 of the Act; the conditions are the same as for personal data but in addition:

- the subject must have given explicit consent for processing;
- the processing must be necessary for the purposes of performing any right or obligation conferred by law, or in connection with employment;
- the processing must be necessary to protect the vital interests of the data subject if consent cannot be readily obtained from the data subject;

- the processing must be carried out as part of the legitimate activities of any political, religious or labour organisation that the data subject is a member of;
- the processing of medical data must be done by a health professional, or some other person with a duty of confidentiality.

Organisations should have procedures for handling requests for personal data and must implement the rights of data subjects under Section 7 of the 1998 Act.

3. What rights do data subjects have?

As a data subject you have a right under the law:

- to request, inspect, and where necessary correct the data held about you;
- to have a summary of the rules that are applied if any special 'computerised logic' or decision-making system is used;
- to be taken off a direct marketing database;
- with certain types of data processing, to prevent your details being processed if it would cause damage or distress;
- in certain circumstances, to obtain a court order to force the rectification, blocking, erasure or destruction of your data (Section 14);
- in certain circumstances, to compensation for inaccurate processing of your data.

You may submit an SAR (Subject Access Request) form to any communications service provider in order to request them to disclose any data that is being held about you and your communication activities. Privacy International is running a campaign to oppose these measures by providing sample letters to the

In the 1970s concern about accuracy of records led to a number of government inquiries into the protection of personal data and on data processing

public. Visit their web site at www.privacyinternational.org for more information.

4. How might data processing threaten civil liberties?

'Record accuracy'
In the 1970s concern about accuracy of records led to a number of government inquiries into the protection of personal data and on data processing.

Nowadays, however, with so many computers being linked together in networks, concerns centre around the uses made of data.

'Data profiling'
Another controversial topic is the 'matching' of several sources of data to provide a complex 'data profile' of an individual. Data matching was first used by companies as a marketing tool, but its use is spreading to government and law enforcement agencies.

'Data Retention'
Under the 2001 Anti-Terrorism, Crime and Security Act, the Secretary of State is authorised to issue a voluntary Code of Practice which could become mandatory if not enough communication service providers volunteer to retain data. Civil liberties groups have criticised the code for allowing the Home Secretary to require companies to store communications data for long periods to allow later access by intelligence and law enforcement agencies. The Draft Code of Practice is open for public comment until 3 June 2003.

- The above information is from GreenNet Educational Trust's internet rights web site which can be found at www.internetrights.org.uk

The Civil Society Internet Rights Project (CSIR) is a GreenNet Educational Trust (GET)-sponsored initiative to provide knowledge, resources and tools for civil society organisations to safely and productively use the Internet as a means of increasing democracy and to campaign on social justice issues.

These materials are produced in cooperation with Paul Mobbs and are licensed under a Creative Commons Attribution-NonCommercial-ShareAlike License.

© *GreenNet Educational Trust (GET)*

Beware when you buy

Big Brother is watching

By Caroline Marshall

Each time you reach the till at the UK's two biggest supermarkets, it's the same question: have you got a Clubcard/Nectar card?

The question can grate, but nonetheless consumers have signed up to these schemes in droves. Nectar card, representing heavyweights such as Sainsbury's, BP and Barclaycard, has more than 11m UK member households (out of a total of 22m). Tesco Clubcard has 10m, while the Boots Advantage scheme tops the lot with more than 15m.

And why wouldn't we fall for these cards? For doing nothing more than the weekly shop we believe we are getting something back. And the retailers? Well, they get us to increase our spending in their stores since we are more likely to shop where we earn rewards.

For the ad industry, the cards are a mixed blessing. The intelligence they gather can provide themes for advertising campaigns and help plan product launches.

On the flip side, in saving retailers a fortune on advertising, they can deprive agencies of income at a time when, as Tesco likes to put it, 'Every little helps'.

Another consumer tracking system is now being trialled by Procter & Gamble in the US and by Tesco stores in the UK. Radio Frequency Identification (RFID), a form of electronic tagging using wireless technology, was developed at the Auto-ID centre in Boston. Big grocers such as Wal-Mart (which owns Asda) and Tesco, as well as brands such as Nestlé, are partners. So is the US Department of Defence.

RFID is a tracking device that uses a chip embedded in the product. Around the size of a speck of dust, it is joined to an antenna. The chip can then talk to a scanning device at a range of up to 20ft.

The conversation between chip and scanner reveals the product's unique electronic code. Each product code links to an internet database entry, so that anyone with access to the scanner can establish what and where that product is.

The developers of these products would have us believe that assigning a unique code to every product on the planet is a goal. Certainly using them on clothes and pricier grocery items that are attractive to shoplifters appears to make sense. (Razor blades, for example, are small, expensive and easily resold.)

> *For the ad industry, the cards are a mixed blessing. The intelligence they gather can provide themes for advertising campaigns and help plan product launches*

To throw a little reality in here for a moment, there are numerous barriers to the wide-scale use of such technology.

The cost per tag is currently 50 cents – five cents is the goal – and the chip only holds enough memory for a day's tracking.

Can you imagine the IT management hassles of clearing out millions (billions?) of tags each day just to gather data on T-shirt wearers' movements? And they may not even wear that T-shirt every day.

Finally, for such a system to work we would need scanners, lots of them. They would need to be installed at every corner, store entry, home, office, school, cinema . . . In other words, they would have to be everywhere, just to notice when an embedded tag T-shirt wearer happens to walk by.

And what do shoppers think of all this? In the US, land of the consumer activist, the Consumers Against Supermarket Privacy Invasion and Numbering, or Caspian (nocards.org) says that the data collected has become a tempting target for legal or political busybodies of all stripes.

As for the UK, the response so far has been typically British: as long as it doesn't harm our children or hit our pockets, we'll accept it with a shrug.

■ Caroline Marshall is editor of *Campaign*.
© *Telegraph Group Limited, London 2004*

Consumer TF270473, "Mr. Bob Mitchell", 48 y.o. Divorced father of two girls (12 and 15 y.o.), plumber, heterosexual, votes Labour, had vasectomy July 1999, partially colour blind, 9 size shoes, fav music: R&B, last year earned £18,000, credit rating: fair

Consumer AF130977, "Ms. Sally Cho" 27 y.o. Single, bisexual, magazine subeditor, suffers chronic back pain, allergic to wheat, vegetarian (eats fish), fav colour: red, drinks café latte (no sugar), last year earned £23,000, credit rating: fair

Consumer GB390476 "Mrs. Jean Roberts" 36 y.o. Married, mother of 2 (boy 3 y.o. and girl 10 y.o.), housewife, takes sleeping pills, reads Harlequin romantic novels, fav. tv show: 'The Bill', secretly seeing a psychotherapist, credit rating: poor

Consumer CS850371 "Mr. Sanjiv Singh" 17 y.o., virgin, left handed, suffers from asthma, fav. food: salt& vinegar crisps, smokes marijuana and cigarettes, wears Nike gear, plays football lives with grandparents. Fav. team: Arsenal

LATEST TITLES

Shopping from home – security and privacy

Paying for goods more safely

When you shop from home, you often have to give more information to the trader than you would if you were in a shop. This could include:

- your name, address, postcode and phone number;
- your e-mail address;
- your credit card details.

Remember that the information you give to a trader can't be given to anyone else without your agreement.

If the company you're buying from wants to pass on your details to someone else, it must also give you the right to say no. This is often done with a tick box on the paperwork. Make sure you do this if you do not want your name passed on.

There are a number of things you can do to ensure more safety when paying for goods:

- try not to give your bank account numbers, credit card details or any other personal information to a company you haven't checked out;
- use credit cards, cheques or postal orders – not cash;
- if you have to send cash, use registered post;
- keep a copy of your order and a note of when you sent it;
- if you pay for a product costing more than £100 on your credit card (even if you only pay the deposit) you may have a claim against the credit card issuer as well as against the trader if you have a complaint. This can be useful if the trader goes out of business;
- if someone uses your payment card fraudulently to shop from home without your permission, you can cancel the payment and your card company must arrange for your account to be re-credited in full;
- if you discover that someone has used your card dishonestly, tell the card issuer as soon as possible.

Junk mail and cold calls

Sellers want to market their products – and to tell you about any new goods and services.

Some consumers don't mind if they receive unsolicited mail, phone calls, faxes and e-mails. But other people only want a company to contact them if they have asked that company to do so. If you are one of those people, there are a number of things you can do.

Unwanted phone calls

If you want to stop companies phoning you at home without your consent, register with the Telephone Preference Service on www.tpsonline.org.uk Tel: 020 7291 3320. Fax: 020 7323 4226. E-mail: tps@dma.org.uk

No company or supplier can cold call someone who has registered with them.

Even if you haven't registered, cold callers must at the beginning of the call:

- give the trader's identity;
- make their business purpose clear.

If they do not, they are breaking the law.

Unwanted faxes

It's against the law for a supplier to send marketing faxes without prior consent. The Fax Preference Service website gives information about this. Tel: 020 7291 3330. Fax: 020 7323 4226. E-mail: fps@dma.org.uk

No company or supplier can fax someone who has registered with them.

The Office of the Information Commissioner monitors both the telephone and fax preference services which are regulated by the Direct Marketing Association. If you continue to have problems you should contact the Commissioner. The Commissioner can apply for an enforcement order if there has been a breach. Failing to comply with such an order is a criminal offence. Information line: 01625 545 745. Fax: 01625 524 510. E-mail: Mail@dataprotection.gov.uk www.dataprotection.gov.uk

Unwanted mail

If you want to stop companies sending you catalogues and special offers, you can register with the Mailing Preference Service. Doing so will remove your name from all mailing lists. You can contact them (UK residents only) at FREEPOST 22, London, WIE 7EZ. Tel: 020 7291 3310. Fax: 020 7323 4226. E-mail: mps@dma.org.uk

Unwanted e-mails

If you want to stop companies sending you unwanted e-mails (known as spams), register with the Direct Marketing Association's e-mail preference service. Their web site is at www.e-mps.org/en/

Please note that this service is run by the US branch of the Direct Marketing Association so any personal data won't be protected by UK laws.

You can also try your internet service provider (ISP) as they can often trace the sources and put a block on future mailings.

What if you receive goods or services you haven't even ordered?

If you receive goods that you have not ordered or that have not been ordered on your behalf, and it looks like the trader has deliberately sent them to you, you can keep them. You are under no obligation to return them to the supplier and it is illegal for a supplier to request payment from you. In effect, you can treat them as a gift.

It is equally illegal for a supplier to perform services for you that you have not ordered and then demand payment.

If a business seeks payment for unsolicited goods or services, they are committing an offence – tell your local trading standards authority.

■ The above information is from the Office of Fair Trading's web site: www.oft.gov.uk

© Office of Fair Trading (OFT)

Data Protection Act

Your rights and how to enforce them

Introduction

This information is part of a series of eight leaflets which explain your rights under the Data Protection Act and the procedure involved if you wish to enforce your rights through the courts.

It gives you general facts about the Act and the body responsible for enforcing it.

Details of our other leaflets can be found at the end of this piece. If you would like any of these please contact the Information Commissioner's Office. You will find our contact details at the end of this article.

Your rights and how to enforce them

The Data Protection Act 1998 (the 'Act') came into force on 1 March 2000. It sets out rules for processing personal information (known as personal data) and applies to many paper records as well as those held on computer.

Many people and organisations (data controllers) have details about us (data subjects). The growth in the use of personal data has many benefits, like better medical care or helping fight crime. There are also some possible problems. It could cause you problems if information about you is recorded incorrectly, is out of date, or is confused with information about someone else.

The Act requires data controllers to comply with the rules of good information handling practice, known as the data protection principles. The principles require, amongst other things, that personal data are processed fairly and lawfully, are accurate and relevant and are subject to appropriate security.

What is the role of the Information Commissioner ?

The Information Commissioner (the 'Commissioner') is responsible for enforcing the Act and for providing advice and assistance to both data controllers and data subjects. The Commissioner's focus is on seeking to promote compliance and the following of best practice. Failure to observe the data protection principles is not a criminal offence. The Commissioner does not have any powers to award compensation to a data subject affected by the processing of their personal data in breach of the Act. Compensation can only be awarded by a court in the event that the data controller refuses to compensate a data subject.

If an individual believes himself to be directly affected by the processing of his personal data, and has been unable to resolve the matter himself with the data controller, he may ask the Commissioner to assess whether the processing is likely or unlikely to have been carried out in compliance with the Act. The Commissioner is not required to come to a firm determination as to whether there has been a breach of

the Act. He is simply required to decide whether, on the information available to him, compliance with the Act is, on balance, likely or unlikely.

If the Commissioner makes an assessment that the processing by the data controller is unlikely to have been carried out in compliance with the Act, the Commissioner will then decide whether remedial action is warranted. If so, he will try to achieve this with the co-operation of the data controller.

If this is not possible, the Commissioner has discretion as to whether to take any action and as to what action to take.

An assessment will inform you as to whether the matters that concern you are likely to involve a breach of the Act. It may help you to resolve a dispute and in making a decision as to whether to take legal action against a data controller under the Act. However, an assessment from the Commissioner is not necessary to make a claim to court.

It is important to note before starting any legal action against a data controller, that an assessment from the Commissioner stating that it is unlikely that there has been compliance with the Act is not binding on a court and the Judge may disagree with the Commissioner's findings. An important difference between an assessment of the Commissioner and the judgment of the court is the evidence upon which the respective decisions may be based.

Further information relating to assessments may be obtained from the Commissioner's website or by contacting the Commissioner's Information Line.

The purpose of this publication and the Information Packs referred to is to identify your rights under the Act and to assist you in solving any problems you may have with a data controller who you think may be processing your personal data in breach of the provisions of the Act. Information is also included to explain how to issue proceedings against a data controller in the County Court.

What rights do I have under the act?

The Act gives you various rights to control the way your personal information is used, including the following:

(i) The right to find out what information is held about you on computer and in some paper records. This is called the right of subject access.

If you would like more information on how to make a subject access request, please refer to the leaflet called *Subject access – a guide for data subjects.*

(ii) If you wish to find out what credit reference agencies report about you and how you correct mistakes on such reports then you will need to refer to our leaflet called *No credit?*

(iii) The right to take steps to prevent your personal data being processed if the processing is likely to cause you or someone else to suffer substantial damage or substantial distress which is unjustified.

If you would like more information on how to take such steps and what to do if the data controller does not lawfully do as you ask, you will find further information in *Help! How can I stop them processing my personal information?*

(iv) The right to require the data controller not to use your personal data to market you with products, services or ideas.

If you would like more information on how to do this and

what to do if the data controller does not do as you ask, you will find further information in: *Stopping unwanted marketing materials.*

(v) Sometimes individuals or organisations will use a computer to process information about you, in order to take a decision that will affect you.

An example of this is an employer who uses computer scoring of job applications to decide who to interview. In some circumstances, you have the right to prevent decisions being taken about you which are based solely on automatic processing.

If you would like more information about this, you will find further information in *Preventing decisions based on automatic processing of my personal information.*

If the decision taken has the effect of denying you credit, you should also refer to our leaflet called *No credit?*

(vi) If a data controller is processing inaccurate information about you, you have the right to have that information amended or destroyed. If you would like more information on how to exercise this right and what to do if the data controller does not do as you ask, please see: *Incorrect information – what can I do?*

If the information which is inaccurate relates to information recorded on the files of a credit reference agency then you will find further information in the leaflet called: *No credit?*

(vii) If you have suffered damage and distress as a result of a data controller failing to comply with the Act, you have the right to claim compensation from the data controller.

If you would like more information on how to do this please refer to our leaflet called: *Claiming compensation.*

(viii) What do I do if I want to issue court proceedings against a data controller?

Where a solution cannot be reached by writing to a data controller, the Act allows you to take legal proceedings against the data controller. These proceedings may be commenced either in the High Court or in the County Court in England, Wales and Northern Ireland or in the Court of Session UK or the Sheriff's Court in Scotland. It is expected that most cases under the Act will be commenced in the County Court or in the Sheriff's Court.

For information as to how to make an application to court please refer to the leaflet called *Taking a case to court.*

The Commissioner and his staff will not usually take any part in court proceedings commenced by you.

The Commissioner is not able to advise on individual cases and their likelihood of success and you are advised to consult a solicitor, Citizens' Advice or your local law centre if you are not sure whether you have a case under the Act before commencing proceedings.

Further information

All the Information Packs and other publications produced by the Information Commissioner referred to in this article may be obtained from www.informationcommissioner.gov.uk

What is in the Information Packs?

Each Information Pack sets out what your rights are and, where possible, includes examples of letters and notices to send to the data controller. You will also find information to help you if you decide to take legal proceedings against a data controller.

■ The above information is from the Information Commissioner's Office's web site which can be found at www.informationcommissioner.gov.uk

© *Information Commissioner's Office*

Towards a privacy law?

Liberty launch investigation into the state of privacy in the UK

Two years ago, Liberty's annual conference launched our drive for a privacy law. Now, with funding from the Nuffield Foundation, the Civil Liberties Trust has commissioned Liberty to conduct a year-long research project reviewing privacy in the UK.

The project brings together key parties with an interest in privacy: government bodies; the police; the press and broadcast media; specialist lawyers; human rights organisations; and academics.

At Liberty, a number of people will be working on the project for the next twelve months: our new Senior Researcher, Caoilfhionn Gallagher, Head of Policy, Gareth Crossman, Campaigns Director, Mark Littlewood, and the Director. In addition, the project has the country's pre-eminent privacy academic, Professor Charles Raab of Edinburgh University, and an expert Advisory Committee chaired by Lord Phillips of Sudbury, a Liberal Democrat peer.

The Advisory Committee, which will analyse and direct Liberty's research, includes Simon Davies of Privacy International, Rabinder Singh QC of Matrix Chambers, Stuart Millar of the *Guardian*, Roger Smith of JUSTICE, and representatives of the Home Office, the NHS Information Authority and the Department of Constitutional Affairs.

The balance between the privacy of the individual and competing interests, such as national security, the prevention of crime, and freedom of expression, has been the subject of debate (not least among Liberty members at our privacy conference) for many years. However, the borders of a right to privacy in the UK, and its relative weight in relation to such competing values, are extremely unclear, and developing in a piecemeal manner.

There are laws which protect some aspects of privacy but disregard

others, including those contained within the Data Protection Act 1998, the Protection from Harassment Act 1997, and the Regulation of Investigatory Powers Act 2000.

The Press Complaints Commission's role in this area is currently under scrutiny; and the rapidly developing confidentiality and Human Rights Act case law suggests that the courts, or at least individual judges, may take action to protect individuals against invasions of their privacy if Parliament does not. Liberty's aim in this project is to comprehensively examine how the state, the press and others currently strike that balance between privacy and countervailing interests, and consider the need for a new approach.

The balance between the privacy of the individual and competing interests has been the subject of debate

---

Liberty will publish its review and recommendations at the conclusion of the project in summer 2004. Our track record on such research projects is excellent. Liberty has worked on other collaborative projects in the past which followed a similar format, and they have had a real impact in policy terms. Liberty's report of April 2000 *An Independent Police Complaints Commission*, for example, is now cited by the newly formed IPCC as one of the catalysts for its creation. Most recently, in March 2003, we produced the report, *Deaths in Custody: Redress and Remedies*, which was widely reported and is currently being reviewed by policymakers. This new project will be the first broad, comprehensive study of privacy in the UK, and our recommendations will benefit from the fact that they include input from key players with very different views.

Details of the project are available on our webpage, at http://www.liberty-human-rights.org.uk/issues/privacy-surveillance.shtml, or from Caoilfhionn at privacy@liberty-human-rights.org.uk.

■ The above information is from Liberty's magazine. For further information visit their web site at www.liberty-human-rights.org.uk

© *Liberty, 2003*

KEY FACTS

■ The UK still has the highest density of CCTV cameras in the world. Since 1994 the Home Office has spent 78% of its crime prevention budget on CCTV, and there are now over 1.5 million cameras across the country. (p. 3)

■ Privacy is a fundamental human right. It underpins human dignity and other values such as freedom of association and freedom of speech. (p. 4)

■ Most Britons say they would welcome or at least not mind identity cards. (p. 7)

■ Yet at the same time large majorities believe that the system would be open to abuse and that personal details held on people's ID cards would probably be leaked to unauthorised people outside the Government. (p. 7)

■ In the eyes of the majority, ID cards would also make it easier for the authorities to track down bogus asylum seekers and people trying to evade deportation. Cards might also prove useful in the war on crime. (p. 7)

■ Large numbers of people suspect that today's credit card fraud would be matched by a new wave of identity card fraud. (p. 7)

■ There is a large majority in Britain in favour of ID cards but they also suggest the hostile minority could turn out to be hard to handle. (p. 8)

■ The Government plans eventually to set up a National Identity Register to hold details of all 60 million people in the UK. Information stored on ID cards could then be checked against the register to authenticate the holder's identity. (p. 9)

■ The cost of the scheme is forecast at £180 million over the next three years, through the total is expected to reach £3 billion after a decade. (p. 10)

■ Other countries and organisations, including the International Civil Aviation Organisation, are planning to introduce similar ID schemes, and from October 2004 travellers to the US will require a biometric visa. (p. 12)

■ Radio Frequency Identification is an automatic data capture technology that uses tiny tracking chips affixed to products. (p. 13)

■ Surveillance is the monitoring of activities of an individual, group or groups of people. New opportunities for mass surveillance are opening up daily with high-speed, networked computers facilitating many of our everyday activities. Surveillance today may be carried out via the Internet, via telephone networks or via the data profiling of individuals. (p. 17)

■ It is carried out for a variety of reasons – by the private sector for commercial ones (such as the protection of intellectual property rights), or by states for security reasons. (p. 17)

■ Does the use of electronic surveillance threaten civil liberties? In situations where data has been used (even where information is erroneous) in a way that damages a person's private life, individuals have limited legal rights to prevent further disclosure or to seek redress for the damage caused. (p. 19)

■ Mobile phone tracking has become one of the hottest new mobile applications. Several services now allow users to track the location of mobile phones, with many making concerned parents their key market. (p. 19)

■ For a switched-on mobile phone, whose owner has given permission, the networks will provide location data with up-to-the-minute accuracy – for a price. You will be able to see the precise location of the base station they are using, and a circle of accuracy within which the network believes the phone to be located. (p. 19)

■ New regulations will give more than 24 state bodies and hundreds of local government officials the power to demand personal communications details, though not the content, of messages and calls. (p. 22)

■ The Data Protection Act can prompt criminal prosecutions and other sanctions against directors, and employees unlawfully monitored can claim damages. (p. 27)

■ Disciplinary proceedings for email and internet abuse at work in the previous 12 months exceeded those for dishonesty, violence and health and safety breaches. (p. 28)

■ Sending pornographic emails was one of the three most common causes for sacking staff – nearly 40pc of disciplinary cases resulted in dismissal. (p. 28)

■ The Data Protection Act gives any individual the right to request to see what information has been stored on them by any data processor, and staff are not exempted from this. Your employer should present you with this information on request. (p. 30)

■ 'Spam' is a general term used to describe Unsolicited Bulk Emails (UBE) usually sent to a large number of email users who have not requested to be contacted by the sender. (p. 31)

■ If you want to stop companies phoning you at home without your consent, register with the Telephone Preference Service on www.tpsonline.org.uk Tel: 020 7291 3320. Fax: 020 7323 4226. E-mail: tps@dma.org.uk (p. 36)

■ It's against the law for a supplier to send marketing faxes without prior consent. The Fax Preference Service website gives information about this. Tel: 020 7291 3330. Fax: 020 7323 4226. E-mail: fps@dma.org.uk (p. 36)

ADDITIONAL RESOURCES

You might like to contact the following organisations for further information. Due to the increasing cost of postage, many organisations cannot respond to enquiries unless they receive a stamped, addressed envelope.

CASPIAN *Consumers Against Supermarket Privacy Invasion and Numbering*
131 DW Hwy.#235
Nashua, NH 03060, USA
Web site: www.nocards.org
www.spychips.com
CASPIAN is a national grass-roots consumer group dedicated to fighting supermarket 'loyalty' or frequent shopper cards.

European Foundation for the Improvement of Living and Working Conditions
Wyattville Road
Loughlinstown
Co. Dublin, Ireland
Tel: + 353 1204 3100
Fax: + 353 1 282 6456
E-mail: mdb@eurofound.eu.int
Web site: www.eurofound.eu.int
The Foundation is a tripartite European Union body set up in 1975 to contribute to the planning and establishment of better living and working conditions.

GreenNet Educational Trust (GET)
33 Islington High Street
London, N1 9LH
Tel: 0845 0554011
Fax: 020 7837 5551
E-mail: ir@gn.apc.org
Web site: www.gn.apc.org and www.internetrights.org.uk
GreenNet supports a progressive community working for Peace, the Environment, Gender Equality and Social Justice, through the use of Information Communication Technologies (ICTs).

Information Commissioner's Office
Wycliffe House, Water Lane
Wilmslow, Cheshire, SK9 5AF
Tel: 01625 545745
Fax: 01625 524510
E-mail: mail@ico.gsi.gov.uk
Web site:
www.informationcommissioner.gov.uk
Works to develop respect for the private lives of individuals and

encourage the openness and accountability of public authorities.

Internet Services Providers' Association (ISPA UK)
23 Palace Street
London, SW1E 5HW
Tel: 020 7233 7234
Fax: 020 7233 7294
E-mail: admin@ispa.org.uk
Web site: www.ispa.org.uk
ISPA UK is the UK's Trade Association for providers of Internet services.

Internet Watch Foundation (IWF)
5 Coles Lane, Oakington
Cambridge, CB4 5BA
Tel: 01223 237700
Fax: 01223 235870
E-mail: admin@iwf.org.uk
Web site: www.iwf.org.uk
IWF was launched in late September 1996 by PIPEX to address the problem of illegal material on the Internet, with particular reference to child pornography.

Liberty
21 Tabard Street
London, SE1 4LA
Tel: 020 7403 3888
Fax: 020 7407 5354
E-mail: info@liberty-human-rights.org.uk
Web site: www.liberty-human-rights.org.uk
Works to protect civil liberties and promote human rights, within the United Kingdom.

Nacro
169 Clapham Road
London, SW9 0PU
Tel: 020 7582 6500
Fax: 020 7735 4666
E-mail:
communications@nacro.org.uk
Web site: www.nacro.org.uk
Nacro's vision is a safer society where everyone belongs, human rights are respected and preventing crime means tackling social

exclusion and re-integrating those who offend.

National Consumer Council
20 Grosvenor Gardens
London, SW1W 0DH
Tel: 020 7730 3469
Fax: 020 7730 0191
E-mail: info@ncc.org.uk
Web site: www.ncc.org.uk
A research and policy organisation providing a vigorous and independent voice for domestic consumers in the UK.

Office of Fair Trading (OFT)
Fleetbank House
2-6 Salisbury Square
London, EC4Y 8JX
Tel: 020 7211 8000
Helpline: 0345 224499
Fax: 020 7211 8800
E-mail: enquiries@oft.gov.uk
Web site: www.oft.gov.uk
The OFT is responsible for making markets work well for consumers. They achieve this by promoting and protecting consumer interests throughout the UK, while ensuring that businesses are fair and competitive.

Privacy International
2nd Floor, Lancaster House
33 Islington High Street
London, N1 9LH
Tel: 07947 778247
E-mail: privacyint@privacy.org
Web site:
www.privacyinternational.org
Privacy International is a human rights group formed in 1990 as a watchdog on surveillance by governments and corporations.

Trades Union Congress (TUC)
Congress House
23-28 Great Russell Street
London, WC1B 3LS
Tel: 020 7636 4030
Fax: 020 7636 0632
E-mail: info@tuc.org.uk
Web site: www.tuc.org.uk
www.worksmart.org.uk
The TUC is the voice of Britain at work.

INDEX

ACKNOWLEDGEMENTS

The publisher is grateful for permission to reproduce the following material.

While every care has been taken to trace and acknowledge copyright, the publisher tenders its apology for any accidental infringement or where copyright has proved untraceable. The publisher would be pleased to come to a suitable arrangement in any such case with the rightful owner.

Chapter One: The Privacy Debate

Nothing to hide, nothing to fear?, © Liberty, *Privacy opinions*, © Guardian Newspapers Limited 2003, *Privacy and human rights*, © Privacy International, *Watching them, watching us*, © Watching Them, Watching Us, *ID cards may be Blair's 'plastic poll tax'*, © Telegraph Group Limited, London 2003, *YouGov poll*, © Telegraph YouGov poll, *The hi-tech ID card built into a passport*, © The Daily Mail, November 2003, *Playing the ID card*, © spiked 2004, *Biometric cards will not stop identity fraud*, © Reed Business Information Ltd, *RFID*, © CASPIAN 2003-2004, *Spy chips*, © National Consumer Council, *Privacy and surveillance*, © GreenNet Educational Trust (GET), *Internet and e-mail privacy*, © Guardian Newspapers Limited 2003, *Eyes on the child*, © Guardian Newspapers Limited 2004.

Chapter Two: Your Privacy Rights

When knowledge is power, © Guardian Newspapers Limited 2004, *New 'snooper's charter' faces legal challenge*, © Telegraph Group Limited, London 2004, *The 'snoopers' charter' explained*, © Guardian Newspapers Limited 2004, *CCTV and human rights*, © Nacro, *Beware secret cameras in the loo*, © Guardian Newspapers Limited 2004, *Someone to watch over the office police*, © Telegraph Group Limited, London 2004, *Workplace privacy*, © European Foundation for the Improvement of Living and Working Conditions, *Monitoring and internet policies*, © Trades Union Congress, *Spam email*, © Internet Watch Foundation, *Spam offences*, © 2004 – Internet Services Providers' Association, UK, *Privacy and data protection*, © Guardian Newspapers Limited 2003, *Communications data protection and retention*, © GreenNet Educational Trust (GET), *Beware when you buy*, © Telegraph Group Limited, London 2004, *Shopping from home – security and privacy*, © Office of Fair Trading (OFT), *Data Protection Act*, © Information Commissioner's Office, *Towards a privacy law?*, © Liberty.

Photographs and illustrations:

Pages 1, 13, 20, 25, 31, 39: Simon Kneebone; pages 9, 36: Pumpkin House, pages 4, 14, 27: Bev Aisbett; pages 23: Don Hatcher; pages 35: Angelo Madrid.

Craig Donnellan
Cambridge
April, 2004